FAMOUS FIRES

Famous Fires

NOTABLE CONFLAGRATIONS ON LAND,
SEA, AND IN THE AIR—NONE OF
WHICH SHOULD EVER HAVE HAPPENED

Hugh Clevely

ILLUSTRATED

The John Day Company   NEW YORK

First American Edition 1958

This book, with somewhat different content, has been published in England under the title *It Should Never Have Happened.*

Library of Congress Catalog
Card Number: 58-9705

For Christine Campbell Thomson
and Ann Elmo

Contents

Contents

Illustrations

All following page 96

FAMOUS FIRES

INTRODUCTION

In this book I am going to describe certain notable fires, and by notable I mean fires in which there were disastrous losses of life or property. One other feature may strike you as being notable about most of these fires. They should never have happened.

Why did they happen? Why do they go on happening? In this age of moral and material progress, when fire fighting is a very highly organized and scientific profession, and most cities and country districts have extremely efficient fire fighting services, how does it happen that 110 people can be killed in a 'fireproof' hotel, or 128 burned to death in a liner lying alongside a dock and surrounded by water? Whom shall we blame when 490 people meet death within an hour in a fashionable nightclub, or seventy-three, mostly young girls, are burned and trampled to death in a large department store?

For that matter, why is it that thousands of people are

being killed and injured every year in the small and unnotable fires which don't feature in newspaper headlines? At this moment a building somewhere is burning. Somebody, somewhere, will be killed by fire today, tomorrow, and the day after tomorrow. In terms of money it is fairly safe to predict that fire damage in Great Britain this year will total at least twenty-six million pounds: in the United States it is likely to be about one billion dollars. During this year, also, several hundred people will die because their clothes catch fire, and two-thirds of them will be women and children. The reason is that women wear a lot of cotton—and cotton, and cotton mixtures, are much more flammable than wool, or silk, or nylon. Men who set fire to themselves do it mostly by filling lighters near naked flames, or by smoking in bed.

The big fires, which occur at intervals, and make headlines in newspapers, do a lot of damage and kill a lot of people. But the small fires, which are almost always unreported, are killing people all the time. So before I go on to the big fires which are the main theme of this book, I want to write about fires in general, and the men who fight them.

If you keep a tame tiger in your house, it is obviously a wise precaution to know something about the nature and habits of tigers. It is especially important to know what is the best thing to do if the animal should suddenly bare teeth and claws and turn on you. But what about that cigarette butt, that small fire left unguarded in the fireplace in an unoccupied room, that electric wiring so

14

cheaply installed? The wild beast hidden in these harmless objects may turn on you, literally, in a flash.

The Oxford Concise Dictionary defines fire as: '*The state of combustion.*' Combustion is simply burning. In order to burn a fire needs heat, fuel, and oxygen. Bring these three together in sufficient quantities, and you will have fire. Take one of them away and it will go out. It will die.

Heat is a form of energy which can be transmitted from one object to another, or radiated into the atmosphere. The heat transmitted directly from the fire in your fireplace heats the bricks of the hearth: the heat radiated from that same fire warms the air of your room. If you have left a garment hanging in front of the fire to dry, the radiated heat may scorch it, or even set it alight. You grill a steak or make toast by using radiated heat from a grill, and if the heat radiated is too great, the steak or the toast will burn.

In a really big fire, the amount of heat radiated is enormous. For that reason you will often see firemen playing hoses on the walls of a burning building where no flame is visible. Their object is to cool the walls and thus prevent radiated heat from setting fire to buildings on the other side of the street. They may also put up screens of water vapor to absorb the heat radiated by a fire, and so prevent it from spreading.

Anything which will burn may be regarded as fuel, though different fuels require different degrees of heat to ignite them. This is clear if you light a fire by using paper, kindling, and coal. The slight heat from a match flame will ignite the paper. The greater heat generated by the burning paper will set fire to the kindling. After that, if your fire is properly laid, the heat emitted by the burning kindling will set fire to the coal. But if your fire is badly laid, with the paper and kindling stuffed in too tightly (thus excluding the inflow of oxygen) the fire will go out.

Oxygen is a tasteless, odorless gas which is necessary to animal and vegetable life, and to combustion. Deprive a man of oxygen, and he dies. Deprive a fire of oxygen, and it goes out. Partially deprive a man of oxygen, on the top of a high mountain, for instance, and his movements become feeble and sluggish. Partially deprive a fire of oxygen, and it smoulders.

From the point of view of the householder, it is the smouldering fire, in a closed basement or ground floor room, which is the most dangerous.

The reason is that a fire breaking out in a closed room will very soon exhaust the supply of oxygen in the room and die down. If there were no oxygen, it would go out. But so long as there is a little air coming in, from under the door for instance, the fire will go on smouldering, building up heat, till everything in that room—chairs, carpets, the floor, even the wallpaper, is at ignition point, yet unable to burn for lack of oxygen. As soon as fresh oxygen is admitted to the room, through the opening of a door or a window, everything will blaze up at once in a great surge of fire which may flash up a staircase and through the whole house.

To illustrate this point I am going to give a brief account of a fire which was not notable. Five people died in it. This was a typical small, fatal fire conforming to the pattern of fires which happen every day in every part of the world.

It occurred in an old, half-timbered farmhouse which had been converted into three cottages for farm laborers. A husband, a wife, and three children were living in the end cottage. This consisted of a living room and a kitchen downstairs, and two small bedrooms upstairs. At the bottom of a short flight of wooden stairs, immediately outside the living room, was a small entrance hall, from which a door led into the living room.

The fire is believed to have started in an upholstered chair about two feet from the fireplace in the living room. The exact cause is not known. It could have been a spark from the fire, or a cigarette left burning.

The whole family was in bed before ten o'clock. Just before two in the morning a neighbor, in the next-door cottage, was awakened by his child crying. He sat up in bed, smelled smoke, and got up to investigate.

Not finding any fire in his own house, he went outside. At first he saw nothing, but the smell of smoke persisted. Looking through the window of his neighbor's living room, he saw a dull red glow. It didn't look to be anything very much, but when he touched the window, the glass was hot. He shouted, and threw gravel at the bedroom window where the husband and wife were sleeping.

The wife opened the bedroom window, and the man

below called to her: 'You've got a fire in your living room.'

She came downstairs at once, followed by her husband. The door at the foot of the stairs was closed. Inside the living room a fire had been burning for three hours or more. An upholstered chair was in ashes, wooden beams were charred, paintwork was blistered, the room was full of black smoke. But the fire itself, having exhausted the oxygen in the room, was only a sullen glow. It needed oxygen.

The woman opened the door.

Immediately, as the oxygen entered the room, a wave of fire surged from the living room, and up the staircase. The husband and wife were killed instantly by an enormous flash, and fumes, mounting the stairs, asphyxiated the sleeping children.

All this happened before the fire department was called, and because a door was opened to the fire.

The lessons of this fire are obvious: (1) If you have an outbreak of fire in your house, call the fire department at once. A few minutes delay may mean the difference between a small fire and a fatal fire; and (2) if you know there is a fire behind a closed door, don't open that door. Leave it to the firemen. They are trained to put fires out.

Fire fighting today is certainly not less dangerous than it was in the days of our grandfathers, but it is far more scientific. New materials used in building constructions, new chemicals, new fabrics, call for entirely new methods of fire fighting. The days when a fireman could be regarded as a man who merely squirted water have long since passed. A modern fireman studies such subjects as the varying effects of chlorobromomethane and carbon tetrachloride as fire inhibiting agents, the effects of high temperatures on prestressed concrete, the flashpoints of industrial solvents, and the hazards of radioactive sludge.

In fact a senior fire officer needs to be a chemist, an engineer, a mechanic, an electrician—and above all he needs to be a fireman. Physical fitness and a cool head are still the first requisites of the professional fire fighter, but for the senior officer they are no longer enough. I once asked a young but fairly senior fire officer why he was a fireman.

'Surely, with all your specialized knowledge, you could be earning more money in industry,' I suggested.

'Maybe.' He smiled. 'Why are *you* so interested in fires?'

'I was in a fire once, and I talked to some of the firemen. After that it grew on me.'

'That's it,' he said. 'You got bitten by the bug. And there's your answer.'

Different fire services, in different countries, have slightly differing methods. But, in general, in a fire station there is a large control room which houses the telephones, radio system, and indicator boards, and also extensive card indexes giving particulars of all streets and important buildings, with details of any special risks attached to particular buildings, and the lay-out and capacity of water mains, hydrants, and other aids to fighting fire.

When an alarm is received a signal to turn out is broadcast through the station, and the first attendance, which usually consists of two engines, is expected to be on the way to the fire within thirty seconds. For buildings with special risks, such as hospitals, or large manufacturing plants, the predetermined first attendance at any fire may be as many as six or seven engines, some of them fitted with special equipment for fighting oil or chemical fires.

On his arrival at a fire the officer in charge of the fire fighters has three tasks to perform. These are, in order of priority:

1. Rescue. To find out if people are trapped inside the building and to get them out.
2. To contain the fire and prevent it from spreading.
3. To attack the fire, *at the closest possible quarters, and* extinguish it.

Never squirt water at smoke, is an old fire service axiom. In any big flare-up, the aim of the firemen is always to get as close as possible to the center of the blaze, and attack the fire where it is hottest. In doing this they risk being burned, gassed by toxic fumes, electrocuted by live wiring, or crushed by the collapse of a wall, or an entire building. (The use of unprotected steel framework in building construction has been a frequent cause of the collapse of buildings in fire. Steel will not burn, but at temperatures of over 600° F. it loses its strength very rapidly, and begins to bend and buckle. A temperature of 600° F. can be reached within fifteen minutes of the start of a large fire.) In a heavily smoke-charged atmosphere, they may have to do their work in stifling darkness, in conditions which would lay an ordinary citizen flat on his back within two minutes.

There are three ways of putting out a fire:

1. By cooling it (taking away the heat).
2. By smothering it (taking away the oxygen).
3. By starving it (taking away the fuel).

Water is the principal weapon of the fire fighter, and it acts as a cooling agent. If a glass of water is poured on the fire in your fireplace, a cloud of steam rises, and a black patch appears in the fire. That is because the effort (or expenditure of energy in the form of heat) required to turn the glass of water from liquid into steam has taken heat out of the fire.

When a fireman directs a jet at the center of a blaze, his object is to force the fire to expend its heat harmlessly in turning the water of his jet into steam. To be fully effective in cooling a fire, the water *must* turn into steam.

If a lot of water is seen lying around after a fire, it doesn't necessarily follow that all this water has been wasted. In a really big fire, where temperatures may run up to 2,000° F., water is the most effective means of preventing the fire from spreading. This can be done by putting a curtain of spray around the burning building, and also by playing jets on neighboring buildings, and so keeping their temperatures below ignition point.

But water is not effective against all fires. Some substances—aluminum dust and magnesium for example—form an explosive mixture when in contact with water.

Others, like cyanide, give off highly poisonous gases. And water will not quench oil or petroleum fires.

Such fires are usually dealt with by 'smothering' them. This is usually done by spraying with chemical foam, which settles in a film over the burning surface, thus interposing a barrier between the fire and the oxygen in the surrounding air. Thousands of gallons of this foam are sometimes used in a large oil and paint fire: at the same time thousands of gallons of water may be used to cool down nearby buildings which otherwise might go up in flames from the effects of radiated heat.

The 'starvation' method of putting out a fire by taking away its fuel is chiefly used in very big or very small fires. If a small chair in your kitchen catches fire, and you are quick enough to throw it out into the yard before the flames can spread to anything else, you are using the starvation method of extinguishing it. The chair itself may burn for a while, but lacking further fuel the fire will go out eventually.

In huge conflagrations, such as that in San Francisco in 1906, or in great forest or brush fires, it may be necessary to blow up whole streets of houses, or burn deliberately large areas of brush or forest to make clear spaces (fire stops) which will halt the onward rush of the flames. This is a drastic method: it is seldom used until other means of fire fighting have failed. If it goes wrong, which sometimes happens, it can easily enlarge the area of the fire.

Every fireman needs steady nerves, considerable physical strength and enough stamina to enable him to maintain an intense degree of effort, over long periods, in almost unbearable conditions. He has to be ready for anything, because he never knows what he may run up against. A fire chief, in charge at a large fire, needs all the qualities of a good general. He must know where to put his men, and be prepared to lead them; he must know where to put up his screens of water vapor to prevent the spread of fire by radiated heat; he must realize when a building is about to collapse, and bring his men out in time. He must be able to think and act quickly. Speed is the essence of fire fighting: a few minutes wasted in the early stages of a fire, or a wrong decision, can make the difference between a medium fire which can be easily mastered, and a conflagration which will burn dozens of buildings.

THE COCOANUT GROVE NIGHTCLUB FIRE

November 28th, 1942

IN 1942 fires were burning, in London, in Berlin, in Moscow. These caused little panic because they were part of the accepted pattern of life in those cities at that time.

In 1942 the Cocoanut Grove was one of Boston's fashionable nightclubs. Originally it had been built as a garage: then it had been turned into a film exchange: and then, during prohibition days, an enterprising gangster had had the idea of turning it into a club. After his murder it had changed hands on several occasions.

Obviously a good deal of remodelling had been needed to turn a bare, utilitarian garage into a fancy nightclub containing bars, dressing rooms, kitchens, a dance floor, and a stage for floor shows. And obviously, since the building was to be used for public entertainments, some precautions should have been taken against fire hazards. This notion does not seem to have occurred to the designers of the Cocoanut Grove when they set about redecorating and partitioning the building.

Immediately inside the new entrance was a small foyer

with, on the left, a narrow flight of stairs descending to the Melody Bar in the basement. Beyond this bar, at the far end of the basement, were the club kitchens and store rooms.

From the foyer, upstairs, a revolving door led into the dance room, which also had a stage for floor shows. Besides this revolving door, there was an ordinary swing door, *which was kept locked.*

Leading out of the far end of the dance room, beyond the stage, was a short passage which gave access to another bar, known as the Cocktail Lounge. Throughout the entire club false walls of thin plywood had been put up to hide the concrete walls and, incidentally, the windows. These false walls were used as backing for a lavish display of palm leaves, cocoanuts, and other tropical vegetation: the décor of the club was designed to suggest a carefree paradise where all one needed was a sufficiency of money. When full, the club could hold about six hundred people without too much discomfort.

That afternoon of November 28th, there had been a big football game between Boston College and Holy Cross, and in the evening it was estimated that about a thousand people had somehow managed to jam themselves into the club. All the bars were packed far beyond their normal capacity: waiters had to struggle hard to serve clamorous customers. The atmosphere must have been truly tropical.

At ten o'clock, just as the floor show was about to go on, a small flame sprang up in a corner of the basement Melody Bar. Somebody shouted: 'Fire!' People rose and turned to look. While they were still looking the flame flared into a blaze: smoke billowed in a thick cloud through the room.

Gasping and spluttering, people rose from their tables and joined in a panic-stricken stampede for the narrow staircase leading to the ground floor. There they packed the foyer and hopelessly jammed the revolving door. A few, avoiding the rush, made their escape quietly at the back of the club through the kitchen quarters.

The progress of the fire was incredibly quick. Flames flashed up the staircase from the Melody Bar, and in a matter of seconds had spread across the dance floor and along the passage into the far ground-floor Cocktail Lounge. Witnesses who survived said that a great sheet of flame seemed to roll in an undulating wave across the ceiling, followed immediately by volumes of thick black smoke. This smoke evidently contained highly toxic gases given off by paint or some other chemical substance. People were found dead who had simply collapsed over their tables: they hadn't risen or made any effort to get away.

Within a minute the whole interior of the club was a shrieking bedlam as people climbed over each other in frantic efforts to reach the revolving door. *But that door was already jammed immovably: the swing door beside it was locked.* In the far Cocktail Lounge there was another door which should have provided an exit to the street, *but this door opened only inwards.* In the rush it too became tightly jammed, impossible to open because of the crowd surging against it. Almost a hundred of the casualties in the club were found lying inside this door. Nobody thought of the windows, which were hidden by the plywood inner wall. This wall was so thin that a fairly strong man could have torn it down with his bare hands.

The fire services were on the spot almost immediately, but there was nothing that they could do except put out the fire and carry out the dead and injured. Everything was over within a few minutes. Of the thousand men and women who had been enjoying themselves in the club when the fire started, 490 were dead and many injured.

As soon as the news of the fire was known the whole of the medical services of the town swung into immediate and efficient operation. A hundred and fifty ambulances were mobilized to carry victims to the hospitals: five hundred auxiliary nurses were called out, and doctors, nurses and medical equipment within a radius of thirty miles came into Boston. In one hospital alone, the Massachusetts General, a hundred and fourteen casualties were admitted between ten-thirty and midnight.

Nobody knows the actual cause of the fire. There was a story that a boy of sixteen replaced an electric light bulb with the aid of a match, and that the match flame set fire to an ornamental palm. This story, which was never proved, sounds like the hasty invention of someone who wants to find somebody else to take the blame. In a club full of people drinking and smoking, anybody might have struck a match and set fire to almost anything.

Another theory was that *cheap and shoddy electric wiring, installed by an unlicensed electrician*, caused a small fire behind the plywood, and that this ignited pieces of flammable material which had been left behind by the people who had run the building as a film exchange. That sounds possible. Yet another idea suggested was that the air of the club was so charged with hot and alcoholic human breath that it formed an explosive mixture (but no fireman believes this one). It seems obvious, in view of the very rapid fire spread, that a lot of heat must have been generated before the flames actually appeared.

What is certain is that the building, with its cheap wiring, flimsy partitioning, high flammable decorations, and inadequate exits, was a fire trap. In passing, it should be mentioned that, in any crowded building, a revolving door should always have a swing door, *opening outwards,* immediately beside it, so that if people want to get out quickly they won't be stopped by a jammed door.

The Cocoanut Grove building should never have been used as a nightclub. Many newspaper writers and public officials noticed this after the fire, and there was a lot of heated writing and talking about it. There were also a lot of funerals.

RINGLING BROTHERS, BARNUM & BAILEY CIRCUS, HARTFORD, CONNECTICUT

July 6th, 1944

In Hartford, Connecticut, the Ringling Brothers and Bailey circus had come to town, and the tents were pitched on a city lot which was used regularly for circuses.

This certainly was a considerable circus. The 'big top,' 425 feet long by 180 feet wide, covered an area of seventy-five thousand square feet, and could hold nine thousand people. The circus itself employed 1,300 people.

On the hot, sunny afternoon of July 6th, 1944, some seven thousand people had come to see the show. Most of them were accommodated around the main rings on tiered rows of folding seats.

The main entrance was at the west end of the huge tent: immediately outside it, and connected with the tent, was a men's lavatory. On the long north side of the tent were three gangways which could be used as exits, but during animal acts these were obstructed by chutes with cages on them, along which animals could be brought from the animals' quarters, outside the tent, into the rings. There were three exits on the south side of the tent: one of these was partially obstructed by electric cables which were led through it into the tent.

Fire precautions consisted of three tank trucks with a capacity of a thousand gallons of water each, and one with a capacity of eight hundred gallons. During performances two circus hands stood by each of these trucks. Buckets were also placed in various positions, and the circus had a number of fire extinguishers which, on this occasion, had not been distributed.

Imagine it—the great high tent, with its tall poles, flags flying, the clowns, the crack of whips, the shouting and the laughter, the gaudy costume of the ringmaster, and on the tiered rows of seats seven thousand people gathered in the stuffy atmosphere on a hot summer's afternoon to watch the 'greatest show on earth.'

Wild animal acts had just been finished in the two main rings: the sawdust-covered center was empty, except for the clowns. A band was playing. The crowd was murmuring expectantly, waiting for the next act to come on.

A small flame sprang up in the men's lavatory, just outside the main entrance to the tent. It wavered, and then seized on the canvas wall of the tent and blazed up a little. A circus hand saw it and threw three buckets of water on it. These had no effect.

The flame mounted, reaching a height of five or six feet, climbing the wall of the tent towards the canvas roof. People in the audience turned their heads to see what was going on, but there was no immediate panic.

There was a small fire: attendants were dealing with it: it couldn't be anything serious. The thought may have occurred to some that one could hardly be trapped by fire inside a canvas tent.

When the fire reached the roof of the tent it was only two feet wide. An ordinary chemical fire extinguisher would probably have put it out in a few seconds. 'All fires are the same size when they start,' is a fireman's saying. This is not strictly true, but it contains an element of truth. *A little fire is quickly trodden out, Which being suffered rivers cannot quench,* was the way Shakespeare put it.

This was a little fire, and nobody put it out. People were arguing, bringing more buckets . . . and then it was too late. A puff of wind came from the southwest, and in a moment the fire was spreading in a great billowing sheet all along the expanse of the roof. The audience, below, saw a raging furnace break out suddenly high above their heads. The ropes holding the big supporting poles were burned through almost instantly, and the poles fell, injuring many people. At the same time the whole of the huge canvas roof came sinking down in flames onto the heads of the audience.

There was a wild turmoil as men, women and children rose, flinging their seats aside, and ran shrieking, trying to avoid the sea of fire coming down on them. These seats, falling in all directions, caused many to trip and fall, thus adding to the confusion. With the main entrance already in flames, a rush started for the northern gangways, but these were partly blocked by empty animal cages: a great mass of bodies was afterwards found in these gangways.

Calls to the fire department were put in by several people who saw the outbreak, and the response was immediate. But, though the grounds were officially recognized as a place for circuses, there were no hydrants inside the area: the hoses had to be connected to hydrants three hundred yards away, outside the grounds.

Before the fire fighters could get into action the whole canvas structure of the tent was completely burned out: it had all happened in a matter of two or three minutes. All the firemen could do was to play their hoses on the blazing stands, and try to extricate trapped people.

The Hartford hospital organization, geared for the possibility of air raid casualties, went swiftly into action to meet the emergency. Within minutes a great procession of ambulances was streaming from the circus into hospital grounds. Those needing hospital treatment were given morphine immediately, their clothes were cut away, they were wrapped in sterile sheets, and injections of plasma were given. Within an hour of the disaster large numbers of auxiliary nurses had been mobilized, and sixty doctors from surrounding districts were treating the casualties.

In this fire 163 people were killed, and 261 were seriously injured. After everything was over, it was argued that only a highly improbable combination of circumstances could have caused the fire. By sheer bad luck it happened that the canvas was ignited, near the main entrance, in a moment when a puff of wind occurred to push it through the tent. That is all true enough. But what big fire is not caused by an unfortunate combination of cir-

33

cumstances? Thousands of people throw burning cigarettes down: most of them go out. Occasionally one starts a forest fire, or burns a house. Plainly it is highly unfortunate when this happens, especially for the people who are burned. Ironically the person who throws down the lighted cigarette is often not among those burned.

There were other unfortunate circumstances in the Hartford Fire. One of them was the highly flammable nature of the canvas roof, which had been weatherproofed with a mixture of paraffin. This, it seems, was the time-honored method of weatherproofing canvas used by circuses.

As has been pointed out by the National Fire Protection Association, canvas can be treated by a process which combines 'weatherproofing' with 'flame-proofing.' Textiles so treated are '. . . *comparatively difficult to ignite, and do not propagate flame, even when in draughts, beyond the area exposed to the source of ignition.*'

163 dead, 261 injured—the figures are shocking. They could easily have been much worse. One favorable circumstance was that the fire broke out during an interval between acts. What would have been the casualties had the rings been full of elephants or tigers when it started?

THE HOTEL WINECOFF, ATLANTA, GEORGIA

December 7th, 1946

THE Hotel Winecoff in Atlanta, Georgia, was different. It was modern, and fireproof. It couldn't burn. The owner lived on the tenth floor. He died on the tenth floor.

The term 'fireproof' applied to any hotel is misleading. Certainly a building may be erected which will not burn. But who is going to stay in a hotel which contains no chairs, curtains, tables, bedding, carpets, or other combustible refinements of present-day living?

The Hotel Winecoff was a tall, narrow building of fifteen floors, with fifteen bedrooms on each floor. Two enclosed elevator shafts and a narrow, non-combustible stairway were the means of getting from one floor to another. Because the place was 'fireproof' no fire escapes were provided from the upper floors, and no sprinkler or fire detector system was installed.

The furniture and decorations were simple, but comfortable. The corridors and stairway had wainscoting of painted wall covering which had recently been repainted; floors were close-carpeted; bedroom doors were of wood with half-inch plywood panels and had wooden transoms over them; baseboards and picture rails were of polished wood. On the night of December 7th, 1946, 304 guests were staying in the hotel.

The fire started in a mattress and some bedroom furniture left temporarily in a third floor corridor. How it began is not known: it may have been caused by a carelessly discarded match or cigarette.

But (as often happens) it must have been smouldering for some time before it blazed suddenly into intense life. A flame sprang from the mattress to the furniture, and in a few seconds was lapping the painted walls that lined the corridors and narrow stairway. As usual, on a stairway, a good draught from below aided the flames.

At ten minutes past three in the morning, a bellboy answered a call to a room on the fifth floor: on entering the room, he left his elevator stationary, with the door open. At three-fifteen, when he tried to leave the room, he was stopped by smoke and intense heat which filled the corridor outside the elevator shaft.

At about the same time a girl was taking some guests to the tenth floor in the other elevator. During her descent she noticed a very strong smell of smoke. She reported this to the reception clerk, who telephoned the fire department at three forty-two. These times are worth noting.

The response was very quick. Within a minute the first

firemen were on the scene and within ten minutes the city's entire fire-fighting force was in action.

By this time the fire was roaring up the narrow stairway, blocking all exits from the hotel. Already frenzied men and women were jumping from the windows. One fireman was killed by being knocked off a ladder by a woman falling from an upper floor.

Various factors aided the fire. The painted wall covering burned with a dense, noxious smoke, which spread through the open transoms over the doors into the bedrooms: more than half of these transoms were found open after the fire. The result was that when guests opened their windows to try to get air, or to call for help, it rushed through the open windows and the transoms, to support the flames.

The fire, burning from the third floor, all the way up the narrow central stairway, could only be attacked from below. For three hours the firemen fought it, forcing their way up those narrow stairs floor by floor.

Many people were rescued by being brought down escape ladders, or by jumping into life nets. Few people were burned by the fire. Twenty-five lost their lives jumping from windows: far more were asphyxiated. In upper rooms men and women were found lying dead, with the furniture of their rooms undamaged except by the smoke.

In all, of the 304 guests in the hotel when the fire started, 119 were killed and another 168 injured. The 'fireproof' building itself suffered little damage. All it needed after the fire was redecorating.

A metal door at the entrance to each floor would effectively have stopped the spread of the fire upwards. Automatic fire detection equipment would have avoided delay in discovering the fire and calling the fire department. A properly maintained sprinkler system would have put out the fire before it became dangerous. A means of escape from the upper floors, other than the one narrow staircase, would have saved most of the lives which were lost.

These precautions were not considered necessary in a 'fireproof' hotel.

THE NOUVELLES GALERIES

Marseilles, 1938

In 1938, in Marseilles, a number of very important politicians, including Messrs. Herriot, Daladier, and Bonnet, were attending a Radical Congress. Many of them were staying at the Hôtel de Noailles, in the Cannebière, the city's famous avenue. A large department store, the Nouvelles Galeries, was immediately opposite the hotel.

The people of the city of Marseilles have a reputation throughout France for being easy-going, happy-go-lucky, and lazy: they take things as they come and don't disturb themselves a great deal. Possibly some of the members of the city council had carried this philosophy a step too far. The town was to pay dearly for it.

The fire started on the first floor of the Nouvelles Galeries at about two-thirty in the afternoon and was caused by a workman repairing a metal fitting with the aid of an acetylene torch, a spark from which set light to a display of flimsy underwear. A garment flared up, and then another, and in a matter of moments a whole rack was in flames. There was a sprinkler system installed in the building which was supposed to come into operation immediately in the event of a fire: unluckily this system was out of action.

Some of the male members of the staff seized portable fire extinguishers which were hung on the wall, and tried to put the fire out. These fire extinguishers were also useless.

Most of the employees in the store were young girls and saleswomen. As the fire spread rapidly from rack to rack in the highly flammable display of goods, all these girls made a wild rush for the door. Four passers-by, a policeman and three soldiers, heard a wild shrieking coming from inside the store. They went in at once, and did their best to control the horde of panic-stricken women. Their efforts were only partially successful, but they did succeed in saving a number of girls from being trampled to death.

Though the Marseilles fire department was notified as soon as the fire was discovered, twelve minutes elapsed before the first fire engine arrived: a second arrived fifteen minutes after the first. Both of these engines might just as well have stayed away: they could do nothing. Their hoses were so old and rotten that they burst as water came through them, squirting streams in every direction except that of the fire.

By this time flames had enveloped the whole building, and were quickly spreading. Then was seen the amazing spectacle of a huge fire blazing in the heart of a modern city, with firemen milling about in hopeless confusion, and thousands of spectators, held back by police, watching the center of their town go up in flames. Other engines began to arrive, but nobody seemed to be in charge: no one knew what to do. Monsieur Herriot, who was then Mayor of Lyons, realizing the danger of a conflagration which might destroy half the town, put through a call to his own fire department, two hundred miles away, and gave orders that the Lyons fire service, with all its equipment, should be put on a special railway train at once and sent to Marseilles.

With no water screens, and nothing to stop its progress, the fire jumped the street and enveloped the Hôtel de Noailles and another large hotel next to it. Nobody could do anything about it: the buildings were just left to burn. An order was given that all shops and buildings near the fire should be evacuated. During the confusion caused by this order, a gang of the tougher elements of the town began looting: a battalion of marines and a regiment of Senegambian troops had to be called in to deal with them. One of the looters even got away with a dispatch case of confidential documents belonging to M. Bonnet.

No real effort could be made to stem the fire until naval fire fighters, with modern equipment, arrived from the port of Toulon, and it was twenty hours after the fire started before the flames were brought under control. In all, seventy-three people, including the manager of the store and the managing director of the Hôtel de Noailles, lost their lives, and many others were injured. The damage to property was enormous.

DROMCOLLIHER THEATER

September 5th, 1926

THERE have been many disastrous fires in theaters, nightclubs, and other crowded places, and in nearly all of them far greater numbers of people have been killed by panic than by fire. It has often happened that one minute the members of an audience have been laughing happily; the next minute they have been trampling each other to death in narrow exits like a herd of infuriated buffaloes.

It has happened too often. Most civilized countries have stringent fire regulations applying to public buildings, and in many instances no notice is taken of them. After a disastrous fire in some building in which, in order to save a little money, these regulations have been ignored for years, there is often a public outcry, with a great number of eloquent and indignant speeches of the 'it mustn't happen again' variety. Occasionally somebody is fined, or even sent to jail. These things do little to console the relatives of those who have been trampled to death, or practically torn to pieces in a mad stampede. Wordy expressions of high moral sentiments are often a gratifying vocal exercise for the orator, and may help to get him re-elected, but they don't raise the dead or put out fires. They don't even prevent fires.

Panic is the real killer in fires in crowded places, and once it really gets started there is almost nothing that can be done about it. Panic is a form of fear, but quite different fom ordinary fear. A man or woman may be afraid and still act rationally: but in a panic the power to think is suspended, and people lose their human identities and become part of a sub-human, animal mob actuated only by a blind instinct for self-preservation. They can't be blamed for what they do, because they don't know what they're doing. If they know what they're doing, they don't panic.

Panic is mostly the result of people being confronted by a risky situation, *and not knowing what to do*. Soldiers on the battlefield seldom panic. In the big fire raids on London and other cities during the war, when everybody knew what to do, there was almost no sign of panic.

In hotels, theaters, clubs and other places of entertainment it is essential that fire precautions should be adequate, and that both the staff and the audience, or guests, should know how to use the safeguards provided. This does not always happen.

Most fires are preventable. They are accidents due to carelessness, ignorance, or even greed. But they are not predictable. After any disastrous fire there are inquiries —why, and how—and usually a lack of adequate fire precautions is revealed. In the Dromcolliher fire no neglect of fire precautions was 'revealed' after the fire. There was no need to reveal them: they were already blatantly apparent before the fire happened. The Dromcolliher movie theater was not a 'fire risk.' It could be described as a 'fire certainty.'

Dromcolliher is a village in the west of Ireland, about thirty miles from Limerick. The population in 1926 was about nine hundred. The nearest fire company was in Limerick.

The theater was in a loft over a garage. To enter it the audience had to climb a wooden ladder and go in through a trap door. There was no other entrance or exit. There were several small windows, with thin bars across them.

On the night of September 5th, 1926, two hundred people were packed into this loft to see the pictures. An operator was showing them. The projection machine was unprotected. The films were on a nearby table, out of their metal cases, and also unprotected. There was a candle burning on the same table.

The performance had just started when the flame of the candle ignited a film. A man took a swipe at it with his cap, and the flames immediately spread to the other films. The operator tried to throw the flaming films out of a window, but only succeeded in spreading them around. In a few seconds the whole of the loft was full of smoke and swiftly spreading flames.

There was a panic-stricken rush for the ladder, in which men and women were knocked down and trampled underfoot. The ladder was jammed with maddened people, all trying to get out at the same time. Under their combined weight, it collapsed, tumbling the people on it to the floor below. But, at least, their lives were saved.

A crowd had gathered outside the theater, shouting advice and yelling for ladders and buckets. But in the complete absence of fire fighting equipment in the village, they could do nothing. Inside the loft everything was blazing, and the air was thick with acrid fumes from the burning film. Some strong men kept their heads. They wrenched away the bars from the windows, and lowered children to the ground. Others saved themselves by jumping, some of them already badly burned. Others, overcome by the heat and fumes, could do nothing to save themselves.

By the time the Limerick fire company arrived the building was gutted. All that the firemen could do was to carry out the charred bodies of the victims. Forty-nine people were killed and many more injured. One entire household consisting of a school-teacher, his wife, a child, his brother and sister-in-law, and a servant girl, perished together.

Both the lessee of the hall and the operator were afterwards charged with manslaughter. They were acquitted.

THE TRIANGLE SHIRTWAIST FIRE

March 25th, 1911

Isaac Harris and Max Blanck were the proprietors of a business called the Triangle Shirtwaist Company, which was situated in the Asch Building on the corner of Greene Street and Washington Place, New York.

The Triangle Shirtwaist Company was what was known as a "loft" factory. There was a great shortage of properly designed factory accommodation in New York in 1911, and many firms had set up factories in buildings designed originally as store rooms or offices. Loft factories were so called because they were on the top floors of buildings, and the reason for putting them on the upper floors was to obtain the maximum light with the minimum outlay for electricity. Conditions in these sweatshops were notoriously overcrowded and unsanitary: the workers employed in them were mostly poor Italian or Jewish immigrants. By working very hard they could earn from five dollars to seven dollars a week.

The Triangle Shirtwaist Company, on the eighth, ninth, and tenth floors of the Asch Building, was a very typical loft factory. On the eighth and ninth floors more than six hundred people worked, girls in closely packed lines at their sewing machines, male cutters at long tables. The floors were littered with scraps of cloth and tissue paper, many of them soaked in oil from the machines. Smoking was forbidden, but the cutters were in the habit of smoking surreptitiously. The top floor of the building consisted of offices occupied by the owners of the factory and the clerical staff.

There were no adequate fire exits. Access to the passenger elevators was along a narrow passage, through which the girls had to pass in single file, and where guards were stationed to look through their bags as they came out to make sure they were not taking any materials away with them. There were narrow staircases leading to two ground level exits from the building, one in Greene Street, the other in Washington Place. The eighth floor doors to these stairways opened inwards, and the door leading to the Washington Place exit was bolted on the outside. This was done, it was said, to prevent the girls slipping out of the workroom for a few minutes' rest break, and thus wasting the company's time.

Certain precautions had been taken to comply with existing fire laws. Hoses and buckets of water were provided on every floor. A steep, narrow iron fire escape zigzagged down the outside of the building into a closed courtyard. This fire escape had not been designed for use by large numbers of people in a hurry: it was quite perilous to descend it at all.

That the Triangle Company was a bad fire risk was

well known to certain people. Fire Chief Edward T. Croker had repeatedly warned the city authorities of the dangers of fire in loft factories. His warnings had gone unheeded. Suggestions to Max Blanck that there should be fire drill and a proper check of fire precautions had remained unanswered.

The Triangle Company was a non-union shop. Only the previous year Blanck and Harris had held out against a demand by the Waistmakers Union for a half day's work on Saturdays. Men and girls were expected to work full time, six days a week.

The fire broke out on the eighth floor of the building at about 4:45 on the afternoon of Saturday, March 25th, 1911. The actual cause was never clearly ascertained. A theory was put forward that it was started by a spark from an electric motor flashing into a rag bin. It could also have been caused by a carelessly flung-down match or cigarette. Whatever the cause, it must have smouldered unnoticed for a considerable time, generating a lot of heat, before bursting into sudden flame.

There had been other small fires in the Triangle factory, which had been quickly extinguished with water from the fire buckets. This one was different. The water flung into the rag bin failed entirely to quell the flames. More drastic efforts were needed, and a couple of men manned the hoses. These were found to be completely rotten, and the valve wheel which controlled the flow of water in the standpipe was rusted tightly and would not turn.

Work stopped as men and girls turned to look. Flames leaped up from the rag bin, and a dense smoke began to spread through the workroom. Men shouted, and women began to scream. There was a scraping of chairs as workers rose to their feet. Then a flame jumped from the rag bin to a long table piled with cotton material and tissue paper and began to run quickly along the length of the table. The rush for the exits began.

Cutters and sewing girls jammed the narrow passages leading to the two passenger elevators in a wild, screaming, struggling throng. But these elevators could scarcely accommodate more than a dozen persons at a time. Others made a rush for the staircase leading down to the Greene Street exit: for a few moments the door to this staircase, which opened inwards, was jammed tightly shut by the press of bodies against it. A policeman who entered the building at the first alarm managed to force it open. His action saved a number of lives.

Others ran for the staircase leading down to the Washington Place exit. There, in the rising smoke and flames, they screamed and struggled and beat vainly against the closed door; and there the fire reached them and killed them, and after they were dead it burned down the door, leaving the iron bolt still shot firmly home on the outside.

The fire increased rapidly in heat and fury, feeding greedily on the highly flammable rags and paper which covered the workshop. Still, on the eighth floor the girls had had several seconds warning. Though many were injured and some killed in the rush for the staircase and elevators, most of them escaped with their lives.

On the ninth floor, where 350 girls were working, thousands of unfinished blouses and paper patterns were hanging on lines. Flames, licking upward from the eighth floor windows, entered the ninth floor windows, and went like a cavalry charge through these blouses and patterns. Within a few seconds the whole of the ninth floor was a flaming hell.

There was little chance of escape for the girls there. The elevators were already jammed, and flames had cut off the entrance to the only stairway leading to the ground. Nor was there any chance of help from outside. The fire department, which arrived within a few minutes of the sounding of the alarm, could do nothing. Their extension ladders would not reach beyond the sixth floor windows; their hoses would not penetrate beyond the seventh.

There was one way of escape, though apparently no one knew about it. On the tenth floor Max Blanck had his office, and that afternoon the two Blanck children and their governess were in the office, waiting to go on a shopping expedition with the father when the office closed. Blanck was warned of the fire by a switchboard operator almost immediately after it broke out. He knew a way of escape. He hustled the governess and children through a trap door to the roof, and then up a ladder to the safety of an adjoining roof which was eight feet higher. When he had seen his family into a place of safety, did it occur to him to go back into the factory and help to rescue any of his work-people? Did he give even one moment's thought to the girls trapped behind that locked doorway? It seems that he did not.

Others did. New York University students, attending

a lecture in the building next to the Asch Building, climbed down from their roof to the roof of the Asch Building and rescued some of the workers on the tenth floor. By this time it was impossible for anybody to reach the ninth floor.

A few girls—about twenty in all—got out by the so-called "fire escape." But within a few minutes that also was useless. Flames, roaring up the narrow well in which it was situated, heated the metal, twisting and bending it out of shape.

A vast crowd, held back by a police cordon, had assembled in the street below. They saw a horrible sight. As the flames seared and bit them, the frantic girls on the ninth floor crowded to the windows, and singly, and then in clusters, many of them with their clothing already flaming, began to jump. A net had been stretched to catch them, but the weight of bodies, falling nine floors, was so great that it simply collapsed under the strain.

In the crowd women were shrieking and fainting: men, cursing angrily, were trying to force the police barrier to get into the burning building. They could have done nothing. Horror-stricken and helpless, the watching crowd saw girl after girl leap from the ninth-floor windows, to be smashed into a bloody pulp in the street below. Within an hour of the outbreak of the fire the bodies of sixty girls were lying on the sidewalk.

In all, 146 girls were killed, and 70 seriously injured.

A shock of horror hit the American public when the story of this disaster became known. At once the question was asked, who was to blame?

The answer seemed to be that everybody was to blame, and nobody was to blame. The district attorney insisted that the State Labor Department was responsible for fire safety arrangements in factories. The governor took the view that the responsibility lay with the Department of Buildings. The Tenement House Department, the Water Supply Department, the police and various other departments, were all blamed on the grounds that while one of them must have had the power to order adequate fire precautions in factories, none of them had done so. The owners of the factory disclaimed all personal responsibility. Hadn't they done all that was legally required? they asked. If it wasn't enough, that wasn't their fault. It was the fault of the city government.

Fire Chief Croker, who had long been urging stricter regulations for fire prevention in factories, said: "I have long predicted such an occurrence. I only wonder it did not take place before. Radical measures *must* be taken to install adequate fire precautions in buildings where many employees are working."

Public indignation was so intense that something had to be done. Blanck and Harris, summoned to appear at an enquiry, were almost lynched by a crowd of infuriated citizens. At a mass funeral for the victims, organized by the Waistmakers Union, more than 100,000 people attended. A sum of more than $120,000 was collected to help the injured and the dependents of those who had been killed.

Equally important, within a short time thirty new city

ordinances were enacted enforcing much more stringent fire precautions in factories.

Blanck and Harris, the owners of the factory, were put on trial on a charge of first degree manslaughter. They were acquitted on a technicality, the judge charging the jury that they could not be found guilty unless it was proved that they knew the door to the Washington Place exit was locked at the time of the fire.

S.S. GENERAL SLOCUM

June 15th, 1904

THERE is something terrifying about fire at sea. A ship in mid-ocean is a kind of prison, even if it is a luxurious prison. No one inside can get out without somebody else's help and consent, unless he jumps overboard. What is even more important from the fire fighting point of view, is that nobody from outside can get in. Fire in a ship at sea has to be fought from the inside with such firefighting devices as the ship carries on board. Luckily most passenger ships have very adequate fire fighting equipment, and many of them employ trained firemen as members of their crews.

Big fires in ships at sea are rarer than in ships in port. There are various reasons for this. Discipline on board the ship is often slacker in port than when the ship is at sea. Workmen may be careless in loading and unloading cargo. The normal sea-going routine of the ship is interrupted. What is surprising is that some of the fires which occur in ships in port are often as dangerous as any which happen at sea.

The fact that a ship is surrounded by water may seem to simplify the problem of fire fighting; but this is largely a false assumption. In contact with water there are certain cargoes which emit toxic gases, others which swell, with disastrous consequences, and others which explode. A heavy accumulation of water in a ship's hold can alter the trim of the vessel and cause it to list dangerously. This not only makes fire fighting more difficult and throws the heat of the fire against one side of the ship, but may make lifeboats impossible to launch. Also, a fire deep down in the hold of a ship is often very difficult to get at with jets of water.

For this reason steam and foam are two of the principal fire fighting agents used in ship fires. The effect of steam, when introduced under pressure into a ship's hold, is to displace the existing atmosphere, and thus starve the fire by denying it oxygen. But steam (unlike water) is not a cooling agent, and a fire 'blanketed' by steam may retain its heat for many days, and flash into flame again immediately as fresh oxygen is introduced.

There have been many appalling fires on ships, with tragic loss of life, and some of these were undoubtedly due to carelessness or culpable negligence. Yet, on a statistical basis, taking all casualty figures into account, the average voyager in a ship is in less danger of being burned to death than he would be in his own home.

The pastor and congregation of St. Mark's Evangelical Lutheran Church of New York set off on June 15th, 1904, on a Sunday school excursion to Forest Grove, on Long Island Sound. For their outing they had hired the *General Slocum*, a large wooden paddle steamer, 250 feet long by 40 feet wide, with twin stacks, set side by side. This ship was well known on the river, as was her commander, Captain van Shraich.

The day was lovely—a really fine summer day; and the *General Slocum*, gaily decorated, steamed off down the river, her paddles churning, band playing gaily, and her deck crowded with women and children in light summer dress. On board were 740 children and 640 adults, of whom only fifty-seven, including the ship's crew, were men.

As the *General Slocum* passed Manhattan's 90th Street a man on the riverside looked at the ship and then looked again. He clutched another man by the arm, and pointed.

'Do you see that? It looks to me like she's on fire.'

The other man said: 'Yes, she is,' and ran to an alarm box and called the fire department. A fire company came galloping up, but there was nothing they could do. Every moment the *General Slocum* was getting farther and farther from the shore. A fireboat and a tug were signalled, and began to chase her.

By this time the *General Slocum* was well in midstream. On the deck the band was still playing: the passengers were talking and laughing happily. It seems that, although the fire was clearly visible to people on shore, nobody on the ship was yet aware of it.

It is not known who discovered the fire. One account, which seems probable, is that a sailor smelled smoke outside a locked cabin, and called another member of the crew. They forced the cabin door open, and the fire jumped out at them.

Almost immediately, in a violent gush of flame and smoke, the fire broke through a forward companionway and spurted upwards to the main deck. The gay strains of music ended abruptly as the bandsmen dropped their instruments. Women shrieked: children cried and clung to their mothers.

The ship was heading into wind; the flames and smoke were being blown towards the passengers. No alteration of course was made, nor was speed reduced: the blazing pyre simply steamed straight on. Afterwards, the captain stated that the engine room failed to obey his signal to turn for the nearest shore.

Writing about the fire, a correspondent of *The Times* (London) said: 'Observers on shore, unable to do anything, were rendered frantic by the pitiable sight presented by the blazing ship. People were clinging to the sides like flies, and dropping off when their strength failed them. Mothers were throwing their children overboard, and some of the men, maddened by fear, thrust aside women and children in their eagerness to get to the rail and jump.'

Attempts were made to put out the fire, but they were doomed to failure from the beginning. The *General Slocum*, though carrying the fire inspectors' certificate of full equipment, *had no means whatever of putting out a fire or saving a passenger*. The fire hose was rotten: the pumps failed to work: the lifebelts were useless, and sank like stones. The lifeboats, such as they were, were securely fixed with twisted wire and could not be moved. Every safeguard against fire on the ship was useless.

The end came when the ship was beached on North Island, blazing fiercely, with the great paddles still turning. There many more people jumped overboard, some of whom were caught by the paddle wheels, which were found afterwards to be clogged with corpses. Others were killed when the main deck collapsed in a welter of flames. Some saved themselves by swimming: some were rescued from the water by a fireboat and two tugs which arrived at the scene, and by swimmers from the shore.

More than a thousand bodies were recovered after this disaster: over half of them were children. Only one member of the crew lost his life—a steward who was drowned because he was 'weighed down with coin.' The captain of the *General Slocum* was tried and sent to jail.

A journalist, making inquiries after this tragedy, asked a shipowner if the life saving equipment on his ships was in good order.

'It has to be,' was the answer. 'I don't bribe the inspectors.'

S.S. *VOLTURNO*

October 9th, 1913

WHEN the *Volturno* left Rotterdam for Halifax and New York on October 2nd, 1913, she carried 564 passengers, mostly emigrants from Eastern Europe, a crew of 93 officers and men, and a mixed cargo of chemicals, oils, straw mats, and wines and liquors.

The weather was very bad. Early on the morning of the 9th the *Volturno* was wallowing in huge seas. But stormy weather in the North Atlantic is not unusual in October: the crew took this as a matter of routine. Only the wretched passengers, crowded into the steerage, were seriously bothered by it. Some of them had never been in a ship before.

At about eight that morning fire burst out suddenly in one of the forward holds, killing four seamen outright in a great flash, and badly burning another. The master, Captain Inch, was below in his cabin when the fire started. He at once hurried to the bridge and saw flames spouting out of a hatch and sweeping across the deck.

Captain Inch gave instant orders. An SOS was sent out;

speed was reduced; the passengers were herded from below and lifebelts were distributed among them. While these things were being done another explosion below disabled the steering and engine room telegraph.

Under the direction of the captain, officers and men set to work to fight the fire. As a first measure they pumped steam under pressure into the affected hold. This was useless: the steam came out through the open hatches almost as quickly as it was pumped in. At that time, with flames gaining rapidly, it seemed likely that the ship would hardly last an hour. Captain Inch decided to launch the ship's boats.

With the ship pitching and rolling in the heavy seas, this was an extremely hazardous business. When the order to launch the first boat was given, some of the emigrants, mad with terror, made a rush for it: they had to be driven back by the crew. Twenty-two people were put into this boat, which capsized while it was actually being launched, spilling all its occupants into the sea. All except four were drowned.

Another boat was launched, this time successfully. Nobody knows what happened to it. It drew away from the burning ship, and neither it nor its occupants were ever seen again. A third boat was launched. This made the water, and floated for a few seconds, and was then swept by a big wave against the stern of the *Volturno*, and smashed like an eggshell. All the occupants were lost.

At this point a message was received from the Cunard liner *Carmania* that she had picked up the *Volturno*'s SOS and was coming as quickly as she could to help. When he received this message, Captain Inch decided not to launch any more boats, but to concentrate on fighting the fire until help arrived. Despite the captain's order, a number of reckless or panic-stricken people *did* try to launch another boat. When it was lowered, only the after end went down, with the result that everybody in it was spilled into the sea and drowned. It was estimated afterwards that 120 men and women were lost in the launching or attempted launching of the *Volturno*'s boats.

Seventy-eight miles away the *Carmania* was steaming at full speed (twenty knots) through a raging gale to the *Volturno*'s aid. Four hours were to pass before she sighted the *Volturno*. During this time Captain Inch and his crew fought to contain the flames in the forward end of the ship.

All this time the ship was being tossed about by the rough seas. The plight of the 444 remaining passengers, huddled together at the after end of the main deck, was almost indescribably miserable. Some were apathetic, swaying like sacks of potatoes as the ship rolled. A party of fifty Eastern European Jews, led by their rabbi, knelt praying and chanting psalms. Their example of courageous resignation to the decrees of providence was not followed by some among the emigrants, who became violent, and had to be dealt with by the ship's crew. Five or six, driven out of their wits, jumped overboard.

At noon, when the *Carmania* arrived, the forward end of the ship was burning furiously. Captain Barr, of the *Carmania*, ordered a boat to be launched to try to rescue some of the *Volturno*'s passengers, but the sea was so rough that it was impossible to get near enough to the *Volturno* to rescue anybody. After an hour's battling, the boat had to return to the *Carmania*, with seven of its ten oars broken.

Other ships arrived at intervals—the *Seydlitz*, the *Czar*, the *Grosser Kurfurst*, the *Devonian*, the *Kroonland*, the *La Touraine*, the *Minneapolis*, the *Rappahannock*. Several of these ships launched boats, but none was able to get close enough to the *Volturno* to effect a rescue. The *Devonian* lost a boat which capsized: the members of the crew were rescued. The *Minneapolis* lost a boat: the crew were rescued by the *Carmania*.

After the failure of the *Minneapolis* boat to reach the *Volturno*, other ships continued to try, and Captain Inch persuaded some of the passengers to jump into the sea in the hope of being picked up by one of the boats. Seventy or eighty were saved this way: five or six lost their lives.

By this time the passengers on the *Volturno* were in a state of utter despair. They had seen boat after boat beaten back, unable to reach them: it seemed that there was no hope for them at all. Big ships of many nations were within hailing distance of them, and could do nothing for them.

At nine-thirty in the evening there was an explosion in the *Volturno*, and flames shot up to a height of seventy feet, putting the wireless mast out of action. Still the crew went on fighting the fire. So fierce was the heat that the brasswork on the forecastle melted and disappeared: even the glass in some of the portholes melted. All that night the ship burned; the heat on the deck became more and more intense as the fire slowly gained headway. All night long the crew of the *Volturno* fought the fire. And all night long boats from the surrounding ships attempted to reach the *Volturno*, and failed, while the passengers crowding the rails of those ships watched with horror and pity, and some of them prayed.

During the night the wind slackened slightly; the sea went down a little. The previous afternoon Captain Barr of the *Carmania* had sent out a general signal asking if any tanker was in the neighborhood. He had received a reply from the *Narragansett* saying that she would arrive at dawn. She arrived, and immediately began to pump hundreds of tons of oil onto the sea around the *Volturno*. This had the instant effect of smoothing the rough water.

A final concerted effort was made by all the ships' boats standing by, and this time, thanks to the oil, it was successful. Five hundred and twenty passengers and crew were rescued by the boats of nine different ships. In keeping with the tradition of the sea, a line had been drawn across the deck of the *Volturno*, with the women and children on the lee side and the men on the weather side. The women and children were taken off first.

Ships of six different nationalities took part in this rescue. British, German, American, Russian, French, and Dutch seamen, all working together to save lives.

In the 11,500-ton *Morro Castle*, passengers were returning from Havana. The *Morro Castle* was a luxury ship. She had cost five million dollars to build. Her length was 508 feet, beam 70 feet, speed twenty knots. Everything about her was sleek and up-to-date. Her fire fighting equipment included smoke detecting apparatus, smothering apparatus, fire extinguishers in prominent positions all over the ship, and 2,100 feet of canvas fire hose.

At midnight on September 8th, 1934, the *Morro Castle* was steaming just off the New Jersey coast on the last lap of her voyage from Havana to New York. She carried 318 passengers and a crew of 240. The members of this crew could not be described as a happy family of well-disciplined seamen, imbued with the ancient and honorable traditions of the sea. Familiar maxims such as: 'Women and children first' would have seemed to them old-fashioned. According to the late William McFee, who wrote a brilliant essay on the *Morro Castle*, many of them had paid money to be taken into the ship's crew because they hoped to make large profits by smuggling dope into the United States from Cuba.

There had been unexpected trouble on this ship that evening—an unhappy event which cast a gloom over the last night's festivities. At dinner the master, Captain Wilmott, who had commanded the ship for some years, was taken ill, and died shortly afterwards. His command was taken over by the first officer, Captain Warms. All public festivities were cancelled, but the bar remained open.

The night was stormy, with slanting rain, and an eighteen-knot wind blowing. At two in the morning the ship was quiet, though not all the passengers were in their bunks.

The fire is said to have started in a deserted writing room: in view of its rapid spread and the great heat engendered it must have been smouldering for a long time. What happened during the next few minutes is a little obscure. It was first reported to the bridge at two fifty-six: a general alarm was sounded through the ship, and the acting captain was summoned.

Passengers, half clad, dazed with fright and (some of them) with alcohol, came pouring out of the cabins. Despite the *Morro Castle*'s up-to-date fire fighting equipment, no attempt seems to have been made to fight the fire.

In a few minutes the ship's structure was blazing like a furnace. A wild shrieking rose from the passengers' accommodations: many terrified people, driven from their staterooms by flames, jumped into the sea. According to a newspaper report, five young married couples joined hands and jumped together. Two of these couples managed to swim to the shore after six hours in the water.

In his office the chief radio operator was waiting for instructions. None came. Incredibly, the blazing ship steamed on, heading into the teeth of an eighteen-knot wind. Other ships in the area saw the fire and began asking land radio stations for information about a 'large ship afire off the Jersey Coast.'

Not for twenty minutes, by which time the radio cabin was on fire, were instructions given for a call for help to be sent. By this time the fire was visible to people on the New Jersey coast.

Other ships stood by to help, among them the *Monarch of Bermuda* and the *President Cleveland*. Eventually the ship was taken in tow by a tug with the captain and certain members of the crew still aboard. The towline parted and the smoking hulk ran aground on the New Jersey coast.

Some of the events which happened on board the ship were described by members of the crew and passengers at a Department of Commerce enquiry which was held after the disaster. A woman passenger gave evidence that she and two of her friends were drinking in a bar shortly before the alarm was given. They saw smoke, but were told by a steward not to worry. 'It's nothing,' he assured them. Taking their glasses with them they went to look, and the fire 'jumped at them.'

An oiler was resting in the petty officers' room after a period of duty which had ended at midnight. He was awakened by a fearful screaming, and found the room full of dense smoke. He opened a door and saw flames everywhere.

'Three times,' he said, 'I started upstairs, and three times my legs were grabbed and I was dragged down as men fought like beasts to get up a narrow ladder stairway.'

The chief engineer was asleep when the fire broke out and did not awaken until the general alarm was given. He then telephoned the engine room that no one was to leave 'as long as man can live there,' and went to the bridge. By the time he reached the deck the fire was so hot that 'not a hundred hoses could have extinguished it.' On the captain's orders (he said) he then left the ship in Number 1 lifeboat, carrying thirty-two persons. Only one of these persons was a passenger. Asked why the proportion of passengers was so small, he answered that 'there were no passengers around,' and he 'guessed they had all been burned to death.'

The first assistant engineer also got away in a ship's boat containing nineteen crewmen and one passenger. In his testimony he said that he did not realize the men in the boat with him were crew: he thought they were passengers.

A New York City fireman who was among those saved gave his opinion that the ship's crew did not understand the simplest principles of fire drill, that discipline was lax, and that nobody told the passengers how to get into the boats.

The acting captain, in his testimony, suggested that only sabotage could have caused the fire and went on to say that 'excessive drinking' may have been responsible for many of the casualties. Some passengers had refused to leave their staterooms after the fire alarm was sounded. Asked: 'Did you have any direct reports of drinking?' he answered: 'Yes, I was told of six young girls who were all very drunk in one cabin.'

Some unexpected evidence was given by the first and third officers of the Dollar Line ship *President Cleveland*, who told the court that they had lost all confidence in their captain, alleging feebleness, incapacity, and delay on his part on going to the help of the burning *Morro Castle*. Later, in a newspaper interview, this captain retorted that his officers had '. . . tried to make a goat of me, but their evidence shows just what they did. They're in the same boat. I took it on the chin here in New York, but they'll get theirs when we get back to 'Frisco.'

There are many stories of heroism, endurance, and self-sacrifice at sea, and the story of the *Morro Castle* is certainly not one of them. In America people were profoundly shocked by the revelations which were made at the court of enquiry. Arguments, charges, and counter-charges about this disaster went on for weeks and weeks. Eventually the acting captain and chief engineer were tried on various counts, and sentenced to two and four years respectively, but these sentences were set aside by a superior court.

134 people were killed in the *Morro Castle*.

September 17th, 1949

THE *Noronic* arrived in Toronto on September 16th, 1949, with a crew of 171 officers and men, and 524 passengers, mostly Americans and Canadians, who were on a pleasure cruise of the St. Lawrence River and the Great Lakes. She was not a big ship (362 feet long, 52 feet beam, 6,905 tons), but her superstructure, in which the passenger accommodations were situated, towered high above the dockside. In this superstructure were four upper decks, labelled A, B, C, and D, which contained staterooms and cabins. The only exit from the ship to the dock was from E deck. Two narrow stairways, port and starboard, led downward through the upper decks to E deck.

On the night of September 17th there had been a good deal of merrymaking aboard the ship, though not all the passengers had taken part in it. Some of them, and some members of the crew, had been ashore.

Fire started in a small locker in the port corridor of C deck, just aft of the stairway leading down to D deck.

This locker contained brooms, brushes, soap, a switchbox containing fuses which controlled stateroom lights, and a large cardboard carton full of rubbish collected from passengers' cabins.

At one-thirty a.m. a passenger noticed a haze of smoke in this corridor as he entered C deck. He traced this to the locker, the door of which was fastened. Plainly this was a matter which needed attention, so he reported to the head bellboy, O'Neil, who accompanied him to the locker. The two of them opened the locker. Inside they saw flickering flames, which did not seem very serious. A small fire had somehow started in that locker: the obvious thing to do was to put it out. No need to make a fuss, or to alarm anybody.

O'Neil got a hand extinguisher and tried to put the fire out. But instead of dying down, the flames came out of the locker and began to spread. Still confident that he could deal with this outbreak without disturbing the passengers, O'Neil then connected a hose to a hydrant, and opened the valve. Nothing happened. No water came out.

This made it clear that the passengers would have to be disturbed. There was a fire alarm system on the ship consisting of a number of boxes in various positions. When the glass on one of the boxes was broken, an alarm bell sounded on the bridge. After this was done it depended on the officer of the watch what action should be taken, and whether a general alarm should be sounded throughout the ship by klaxons controlled from the pilot house.

O'Neil broke the glass in one of these alarms, and the captain of the ship was notified of the fire. He investigated, and found some of the cabins on C deck were now ablaze, and smoke and flames were spreading rapidly. The general alarm was sounded, and the captain and another officer went to try to arouse the sleeping passengers by banging on their cabin windows.

Some were already awake and crowding into the narrow passages yelling for help. Others, wakened by the yelling, took no notice of it at first. They thought it was merely another party continuing in somebody's cabin.

A twelve-knot wind was fanning the flames, which spread right across the deck, blocking the two narrow stairways and driving the terrified passengers upwards. A press photographer, on his way home from his office, saw the flames, and heard a long and horrible screaming which rose above the roar of the fire. On the upper decks of the ship terrified men and women were fighting to get at ropes and ladders dangling from the ship's side. Some of them, their night clothes blazing, jumped into the water.

At this stage, *fourteen minutes after the discovery of the fire, no alarm had yet been sent in to the fire department.*

A dock watchman, seeing flames break out of portholes in the stern of the ship, telephoned the fire department: the first engines arrived within three minutes.

Firemen found the three top decks of the ship blazing fiercely. Through the flames and smoke they could see, on B deck, a number of passengers in the bows.

While some firemen ran out the hoses, others quickly extended an eighty-foot ladder from the dock side to B deck. This first rescue attempt had an unhappy ending.

As the ladder touched the deck, there was a rush of passengers towards it and eight or nine people tried to scramble on to it at the same time. The ladder broke, and six people fell into the water. They were rescued.

As the fire department went into action, more ladders were pitched against the ship's side, and high pressure jets were brought to play on the flames. Firemen, battling their way with axes through splintered woodwork, penetrated many upper cabins, rescuing passengers and lowering them to the dock side. Long lines of ambulances took them away.

For two hours the battle went on in the blazing superstructure before the flames were brought under control. The ending of the fight was ironic. As the last flames died down in the mass of rubble, melted glass, and twisted steel plates, the ship sank quietly at the dock side, only the remains of her battered superstructure still sticking up out of twenty-eight feet of mud and water.

Of the ship's passengers, 128 lost their lives.

THE *HINDENBURG*

May 6th, 1936

FOR some years after World War I there was a division of opinion among experts about the future of commercial flying. One school of thought favored the heavier-than-air biplane or monoplane: the other favored the lighter-than-air dirigible.

Those favoring the dirigible put forward emphatic claims on its behalf. The airplane, they conceded, was more suited to military flying than the dirigible, being faster, more maneuverable, and less vulnerable to attack. But for peacetime and commercial flying, they contended, the advantages of the dirigible were outstanding. It had far greater comfort, reliability, load-carrying capacity, and endurance than the airplane, and it could fly safely in conditions of poor visibility that would ground any heavier-than-air aircraft.

Performances seemed to substantiate these claims. In July 1919, the British dirigible *R 34* made the first two-way crossing of the Atlantic. In 1924 the Zeppelin *LR 11*, subsequently christened the *Los Angeles*, flew from Germany to the U.S.A. In 1926 an Italian airship, under the leadership of Captain Amundsen and General Nobile, flew to the North Pole. In 1929, following many long flights, mostly by German-built dirigibles, the *Graf Zeppelin* flew around the world.

There were also mishaps and setbacks. In 1921 the *R 34* was destroyed at her mooring mast during a violent gale: there was no loss of life. The U. S. Navy dirigible *Shenandoah* crashed into the sea in 1925, killing fourteen of her crew. In 1930 the great British dirigible *R 101*, while on a 'prestige' flight to India, crashed into a hillside in France, killing forty-seven people, including a number of high air ministry officials. In 1933 the U. S. Navy ship *Akron* crashed in a thunderstorm, killing seventy-three, and two years later her sister ship, the four-million-dollar *Macon*, fell into the Pacific: nearly all of her crew were saved.

These were all accidents to military airships. To offset them the lighter-than-air enthusiasts could point out that no dirigible engaged on passenger service had ever had any serious accident, or killed a passenger. This proud record was to be maintained until 1937.

The *Hindenburg*, the greatest airship ever built, was designed to be a 'safe' ship, the first of a number of giant Zeppelins which, it was planned, would operate regularly over the Atlantic. In her 803 feet long envelope (nearly two hundred feet longer than the passenger liner, *Morro Castle:* see page 64) she carried a volume of 7,300,000 cubic feet of gas. Motive power was provided by four sixteen-cylinder Daimler-Benz Diesel engines of 1,100 horse power each. Her cruising speed, in still air, was eighty-four miles per hour. Her range was sufficient for a two-way crossing of the Atlantic without refuelling, though this was never done.

The big gas-bag was filled with hydrogen, which is highly inflammable when in contact with air. Helium, which is non-inflammable, would have been better, but there was no helium available. The only country producing helium was the United States, and in view of the international situation (Hitler had already occupied the Rhineland) the U. S. had none for sale to foreign aircraft manufacturers.

But the *Hindenburg* was regarded as a 'safe' ship—the safest dirigible ever made. Every precaution was taken against a possible outbreak of fire. Passengers were encouraged to believe that they could travel, not only in complete safety, but in speed and comfort.

There could be no doubt about the speed or comfort. The *Hindenburg*, although on a smaller scale, had every amenity provided in a first-class passenger liner—dining room, bar, saloon, promenade decks, staterooms. Letters could be written and mailed on board. There was even a smoking room, insulated from the remainder of the ship by double doors, one of which had to be closed whenever the other was open. Smoking on board was not allowed except in this smoking room.

On May 6th, 1936, the *Hindenburg* took off from Friedrichshaven on her first transatlantic crossing, carrying fifty-one passengers, and a crew of fifty-six. The trip was uneventful, and on her arrival the *Hindenburg* received a tumultuous welcome from a huge crowd assembled to meet her.

Nine more successful crossings were made during the summer of 1936; and it seemed that all the optimistic prophecies about the future of lighter-than-air transport across the Atlantic had been fully justified. Everything was going like clockwork.

During the winter of 1936-7 the *Hindenburg* switched from the North Atlantic to the South Atlantic route, making several trips to South America.

In 1937 the *Hindenburg* resumed the North Atlantic crossing, taking off on May 2nd, for the first trip of the season with a total of ninety-seven crew and passengers on board. The flight across was uneventful, but rather slow: headwinds reduced the airship's speed a little. At about three in the afternoon of May 6th, when she arrived over New York, she was several hours behind schedule. She should have moored at Lakehurst, New Jersey, at eight in the morning.

The big airship circled over New York at low altitude, her engines throbbing gently: below in the streets heads were upturned to watch. This first trip of the year was something of an occasion, and the *Hindenburg* was showing herself—displaying her immense silver cigar-shaped length, with the black Swastikas painted on the fins, as an advertisement of what Hitler's Reich could accomplish.

At Lakehurst large crowds had been waiting since early morning. A radio broadcast of the ship's arrival had been arranged. Reporters and cameramen were on the spot, ready: friends and relatives were growing impatient. But Captain Max Preuss, in command of the *Hindenburg*, was in no great hurry.

This was Captain Preuss's first trip as commander on a North Atlantic flight, though he had commanded the ship on other flights. With him, as 'adviser,' was Captain Lehmann, a former commander of the *Hindenburg*. Both of these men were highly experienced commanders.

At about four in the afternoon the airship was sighted approaching Lakehurst, and the wearied relatives and reporters sighed with relief. Captain Preuss did not like the look of some dark thunder clouds which were coming up, and signalled that he was delaying his landing until the weather was clearer. He hoped to moor at about six-thirty.

For two and a half hours the *Hindenburg* circled, while a violent thunderstorm deluged the ground with rain. Just before seven the weather, had cleared slightly and cloud base was at 2,500 feet. The *Hindenburg* signalled that she was coming in.

There was nothing unusual in all this. Nobody foresaw any trouble, least of all Captains Preuss and Lehmann. There had been a delay, but delays are not infrequent in any form of transportation. Now they were coming in to moor, as they had done successfully on countless previous occasions.

Below, the ground crew took up their positions near the mooring mast. People were taking photographs: the radio commentator had begun his transmissions: customs and immigration officials were ready to interview the passengers. Everything was set for a routine landing.

The *Hindenburg* drew closer, making a tight turn as she came in to counteract a sudden change of wind. At seven-twenty, from a height of 150 feet, she dropped two landlines. These were picked up by the ground crew and made fast to 'mooring cars' which were on the circular track around the mooring mast.

Aboard the airship, a number of passengers were packing final items: others were lining the windows of the promenade deck, trying to pick out acquaintances, and waving to people below.

Everything then happened very quickly, so that eye-witness accounts of the events of the next two minutes vary slightly in detail.

The huge bulk of the airship floated down slowly to a height of seventy-five feet from the ground, hovering at a point just short of the mooring mast. It seems that she had had a shade too much forward speed. Captain Preuss gave an order to the engineers to reverse the direction of rotation of the propellers, thus providing braking effect, and shouted to the ground crew to pay out landline. Only one of the ground crew heard this order. The result was that, with one line loose and one fast, the airship was thrown slightly off balance.

This was not important. Watching experts considered that, even if Captain Preuss's approach on this occasion was not the best he had ever made, there was still no serious error of judgment in it. And, at that moment, about seven twenty-four, everything appeared to be quite normal. Already radio messages were being sent announcing the safe arrival of the *Hindenburg*. The voice of the radio announcer was calm and unexcited. (I heard the broadcast.)

The ground crew, looking upwards, saw a sudden flash of flame in the airship, just aft of the port gondola, near the tail-end of the ship. In a moment the whole tail-end of the ship was in flames. Someone shouted: 'Run for your lives,' and the ground crew scattered in all directions to escape the blazing mass which was coming down on them. At his microphone the radio reporter went into near-hysteria. 'It's terrible . . . terrible . . .' he gasped.

It *was* terrible.

As flames flashed swiftly up the whole length of the gas-filled envelope, the tail of the aircraft dipped to the ground, while the nose rose in the air. Quite gently, with an enormous fountain of fire spouting upwards, the ship began to sink down lower and lower onto its collapsing tail. From the windows on the promenade deck passengers were already jumping. Some jumped from too great a height and killed themselves. Others were killed by the blazing mass coming down on top of them.

A ship's cabin boy just missed this fate: he had a miraculous escape. He jumped to the ground, but was overpowered by the heat. At the last moment, as consciousness was leaving him, one of the airship's water tanks burst, spilling the whole of its contents down on him. He was able to get up and stagger out of danger.

The *Hindenburg* settled in a vast mass of flaming

wreckage. It seemed almost impossible that anybody could be saved from it. But out of this wreckage men and women came reeling, some badly burned, some with their clothes on fire, and some, miraculously, almost untouched. They were helped by the ground crew, and by spectators who went in as close to the wreckage as the heat would permit.

On the bridge, forward, the two Captains, Preuss and Lehmann, stuck to the ship till the last possible moment. They jumped from a height of about twenty feet, and both managed to struggle out of the flames, their clothes burning furiously. As he was picked up, and put into an ambulance, Captain Lehmann was heard to keep muttering: 'I don't understand it: I don't understand it.' Later, in the hospital, he stated that the fire must have been due to sabotage. He died the following day.

The cause of the fire was never clearly established. One theory was that a spark from the exhausts might have ignited a slight escape of gas. Another theory, put forward by Dr. Eckener, the designer of the airship, and quoted by Thor Neilson in his book, *The Zeppelin Story*, was that the tight turn made while coming in to the mooring mast had set up stresses in the hull which broke a bracing wire. This wire lashed back, cutting open a gas cell. There had just been a thunderstorm: the air was full of static electricity. When the landing line hit the ground, this caused a spark which ignited the escaping gas.

Thirteen passengers and twenty-two members of the airship's crew met their deaths in this disaster: many others were badly burned. These were the first paying passengers ever to lose their lives in a disaster to a dirigible. They were also the last.

When the accident to the *Hindenburg* occurred, a sister ship was under construction at Friedrichshaven, and there were plans to build two more big dirigibles in America. None of these ships was ever completed. The accident to the *Hindenburg* had settled the heavier-than-air or lighter-than-air controversy in five minutes. The dirigible as a means of transport was dead.

An explosion is a quick fire. It is a very quick fire, in which total combustion takes place, literally, with a bang. Or, to put it in a few words, it is a very rapid release of energy in the form of heat accompanied by a large volume of expanding gases. This violent expansion of gases in an explosion causes the 'blast' which can knock buildings over.

Volumes could be written about the differing characteristics of various explosives. For the purpose of this chapter I shall divide explosives into two classes—gases and solids. There are certain gases which become explosive when diluted with a suitable proportion of the oxygen in the air. Coal gas is a notable example. If you leave a gas stove on, without lighting it, and then, after an interval, strike a match, the result will be an explosion. There have been many such small explosions causing loss of life.

Certain highly volatile liquids give off vapor which becomes highly explosive when in contact with the oxygen in the air. Refined gasoline is the best known of these. One gallon of this product, vaporized and mixed with air in a carburetor and introduced in small quantities by means of an induction pipe into the cylinder head of an internal combustion engine, and there ignited by a spark, will generate enough energy to propel a heavy car a distance of from twenty to thirty miles (depending on the car and the driver).

Petroleum products must be vaporized and mixed with air in order to explode. A peculiarity of the solid explosives is that they can explode quite independently of the oxygen in the air. They are 'oxygen carriers' and contain in their own substance all the oxygen they need for swift combustion. They are also sensitive to varying degrees of shock as well as to heat. Some will explode if dropped. Others require the explosion of a detonator to set them off.

The distinguishing feature of explosions is the rapidity with which they develop enormous pressure through the violent expansion of gases, and the extent of immediate damages which may be done by the resultant shock wave. There are no means of fighting an explosion, because everything is over in a moment, except the task of fighting secondary fires, sorting out the ruins, and burying the dead. All that can be done about explosions is to take the strictest precautions to ensure that they don't happen.

Bombay, the gateway to India from the West, is a large, tawdry city with a horrible climate and few imposing buildings. In 1944 it was smelly, noisy, and over-crowded.

The seven-thousand-ton ship *Fort Stikene* arrived in Bombay harbor on April 13th, 1944. Her cargo consisted principally of 1,395 tons of high explosives, and a large quantity of cotton.

In normal times, with such a dangerous and curiously mixed cargo, she would have berthed in a special dock, away from other shipping. Because of the war she berthed in the ordinary commercial dock, and began to discharge her cargo. Many other ships were discharging cargo at the same time.

Shortly after midday on April 14th, smoke was seen coming from a lower hold, where cotton was stacked. A ship's officer was told. Hoses had already been rigged on board the ship in compliance with local regulations, and water was at once pumped into the hold. This had no effect.

The Bombay Fire Department was then notified, and it sent two pumps and an auxiliary tender to deal with what it imagined was going to be a small fire. More water was pumped into the hold, but little seems to have been done to locate the actual seat of the fire.

As a result of the large quantities of water which had been pumped in, the hold became flooded. At about three o'clock it was noticed that smouldering bales of cotton, rising on the surface of the water, were approaching the hold above, where quantities of T.N.T. were stored.

This caused some excitement: more fire engines were called. There were arguments and deliberations. Men were sent for from a local engineering plant and an attempt was made to reach the seat of the fire by cutting a piece out of the plating of the ship's side. While this was being done, water was sprayed over the cases containing T.N.T. to keep them below ignition temperature.

Despite all these efforts, heat in the burning hold continued to increase. Smoke and steam hung in a cloud over the ship. In this smoke men worked frantically trying to keep flames away from the T.N.T. A small flame sprang up and was extinguished and then another. And still the heat continued to increase.

Just after four o'clock an order was given to abandon the ship and clear the area. Men laid down their hoses and turned, prepared to withdraw. They were too late.

There was a tremendous explosion which blew the stern right off the ship, killed forty firemen outright, and set fire to several ships in the vicinity. A huge wave surged across the harbor, splashing against the dock sides. Another ship, the *Jalapadma*, was wrenched from her moorings and crashed into the *Fort Stikene*.

Dockside sheds were smashed into rubble by the force of the explosion. All over the harbor ships caught fire. In a thick haze of dust and smoke, which enveloped everything, men did not know what they were doing. Alarm sirens sounded, and people came running from their homes, thinking that there was an air raid.

Then came a second, and worse explosion, which shot burning fragments a thousand feet into the air and blew the *Fort Stikene* and *Jalapadma* into pieces. Flames swept right across the harbor as more than twenty ships, torn from their moorings, surged helplessly in the swell caused by the explosions. Burning fragments, hurled through the air, started several fires in the flimsy residential districts round the dock area. The whole surface of the harbor was dotted with bales of burning cotton.

The entire fire-fighting force of Bombay was mobilized, and troops were called in to deal with the blaze and to clear away the wreckage. The port area had to be cordoned off while they fought the blaze. For twenty-four hours they worked, fighting the fire, rescuing the injured, bringing out the dead in a fog of heat and thick smoke. When the smoke finally cleared the harbor area looked as if it had sustained a major bombing raid with the shattered hulks of nineteen ships grotesquely littering the harbor.

Little was written in the world's press about this disaster because of wartime censorship. Bombay went into mourning for nine hundred dead and more than two thousand injured.

In one place a vessel four hundred feet long, with a dead weight of four thousand tons, was lifted bodily over a fifty-foot-high building and deposited flaming on the quayside, its bow overhanging the water. An area of over a hundred acres was gutted. After the explosions bulk grain stores continued to smoulder for four months. The monetary loss was estimated at eighty million dollars.

THE TEXAS CITY EXPLOSION

April 16th-17th, 1947

THREE years after the Bombay explosion a seven-thousand-ton ship put into Texas City, Texas, harbor and was berthed in the Texas City Railroad Company's docks. This was the S.S. *Grandcamp*, owned by the Compagnie Générale Atlantique. She carried a crew of seven officers and thirty-two men, and her mixed cargo included peanuts, cotton, oil-well machinery, and ammunition. In Texas City she was to take on board a further cargo of ammonium nitrate fertilizer.

The word 'fertilizer' has a reassuring and harmless sound, reminiscent of green vegetables and fields of waving corn. But add the words 'ammonium nitrate' and pack this fertilizer into the hold of a ship, and you have one of the most terrifying fire hazards in existence.

The docks in Texas City are not, as in London or New York, within a stone's throw of residential property. They are in a wide area owned by oil companies, chemical plants, and other industrial concerns.

When work stopped on the evening of April 5th,

1947, 1,400 tons of fertilizer had been loaded into the holds of the *Grandcamp*. Work started again at eight the following morning.

A few minutes after eight, four men were loading ammonium nitrate into one of the lower holds; four other men were standing waiting. It is said that one of the waiting men lit a cigarette.

At eight-fifteen smoke was seen in the hold. Something was burning, and a hasty attempt was made to put it out by pouring drinking water on it. This had no effect: the volume of smoke only increased. A ship's officer was called.

On his instructions, everyone was ordered out of the hold, and a fire hose was manned. Then the mate gave orders that no jets of water should be used, for fear of damaging the cargo. The hold was closed, and steam was introduced to blanket the fire.

At eight-thirty the fire department was called and four fire trucks arrived within a few minutes. The crew was ordered off the ship and assembled on the dock side. Fire fighters went into the ship, trying to penetrate through clouds of thick, orange-brown smoke, into the lower hold.

At twelve minutes past nine the ship suddenly exploded.

More than four hundred people, including most of the firemen, were killed outright by this explosion. Sheds were levelled; the Monsanto Chemical Works flamed up in a huge fire. Two small aircraft which happened to be flying overhead were literally blown out of the sky: their occupants were killed. An enormous wave, surging across the harbor, lifted a steel barge and deposited it a hundred feet inshore. The S.S. *High Flyer* was blown right across the slip, and came into violent collision with the S.S. *Wilson B. Keene.* Members of both these ships' crews were injured. These ships had to be abandoned by their crews.

Calls for help were sent out, and fire-fighting, Army, and Red Cross units were rushed to the area. They had to work in almost impossible conditions. Flames were raging everywhere; burning wreckage littered the ground; and thick smoke, heavily charged with the fumes of burning chemicals, made seeing and breathing extremely difficult. People had to be warned not to approach the fire area without gas masks.

All that day the fight against the fire went on, and it seemed to be a hopeless battle. With vast quantities of highly combustible fuel to feed on, the fire leaped up again as quickly as it was subdued. At six-twenty in the evening flames from a burning warehouse spread to the damaged *High Flyer* and *Wilson B. Keene*, which were still jammed together after their collision. The *High Flyer* had on board a cargo which included both sulphur and nitrate.

For hours, battling in thick fumes, fire fighters made heroic efforts to move these ships away from the dock. Their efforts were unavailing. At twelve fifty-five on the morning of the 17th, orders had to be given to the firemen to withdraw.

This withdrawal was barely in time. At ten minutes

past one the *High Flyer* and *Wilson B. Keene* blew up in a series of huge explosions which shook the houses of Galveston, twelve miles away. In one area, some distance from the docks, four big oil storage tanks went up in great spouts of flame, to be followed immediately by four others. Reinforced concrete warehouses, normally fire-resistant, were simply blown apart and reduced to crumbling fragments of masonry. When morning came the sunlight was dimmed by a vast pall of oily smoke, which hung like a cloak over Texas City.

Two days were to pass before the fire was finally brought under control. The total number of dead is difficult to assess, because many who were killed in the explosion were migrant workers who simply vanished without trace. The total number killed has been estimated at a thousand, with four thousand injured.

Material damage was done to the extent of sixty-seven million dollars.

THE OHIO STATE PENITENTIARY

April 21st, 1930

Silent Cal Coolidge (the business of America is business) had been replaced as President by Herbert Hoover (prosperity is just around the corner). By this time prosperity was well round the corner and getting farther and farther away every day.

Young men leaving universities and technical colleges found no jobs waiting for them. Husbands who had furnished their homes on the installment system were out of work and could not meet the payments. Crime was on the increase, and all the jails were overcrowded.

The Ohio State Penitentiary, in Columbus, Ohio, was one of the most overcrowded. Built early in the nineteenth century, when the population was smaller and crime was less rampant, it had been designed to hold 1,500 prisoners.

On April 21st, 1930, there were 4,300 convicted criminals inside this jail. This was far too many for anybody's comfort. It wasn't even sanitary. Work was going on to enlarge the building. An extension was being added to a six-story block, and a maze of scaffolding had been erected. The fire started in this scaffolding.

There are different stories about the origin of the fire. One story is that it was started by a blowtorch handled by one of the workmen. Another story, put forward by some of the prison guards, was that the fire was deliberately started by prisoners to cover an attempt to escape.

The first alarm sounded at six o'clock, when prisoners were being locked into their cells for the night. On the top floor of the prison, many of them had already been locked in.

When the first alarm sounded, there was a certain amount of commotion. Prison guards turned out, but nobody seemed to know what to do. Anyway, there was no cause for alarm. The prison was known to be fireproof.

Flames mounted through the scaffolding, blackening the wall of the adjacent block. Timber blazed, and a column of smoke arose as the flames mounted higher and higher. Inside the prison the guards were nervous and agitated, impatient to get the prisoners safely out of the way, into the cells.

Flames spread from the top of the scaffolding to the prison roof. The roof of this 'fireproof' prison was made of wood covered with a preparation of tarred paper. A strong wind fanned the flames.

Within minutes the fire spread right across the roof. Inside the prison a furious fight had started, the prisoners not yet shut up shouting and struggling, the armed guards trying to push them into their cells.

One of the regulations in the Ohio State Penitentiary was that the prisoners should be locked in at six o'clock. Fire or no fire, in the absence of orders to the contrary, the guards intended to enforce this regulation. When a prisoner seized a chisel and tried to force a cell door open to release other prisoners, a guard shot him dead.

Everything was confusion in the long, grim door-lined corridor as prisoners and guards, cursing and shouting, struggled in the thickening smoke. Into this confusion a messenger from the warden's office forced his way, shouting an order that the cell doors were to be opened. Then it was found that somebody had lost the keys.

Large sections of the roof were caving in, turning each cell into a separate furnace. Behind the locked doors men were screaming, beating with their fists against the steel, and dying. When the keys were found some of the cell doors were already so hot that the locks were warped and the keys would not fit.

Sledge hammers and crowbars were sent for, and prisoners, working heroically in the smoke and heat, battered ineffectively with them at the heavy steel doors. From other cells, away from the fire, other prisoners were released: nearly four thousand of them were herded together in a surging crowd under the guns of the guards in the prison yard. A riot started, the maddened prisoners attacking indiscriminatingly both the prison guards and firemen trying to enter the prison to deal with the flames.

More fires were started by prisoners hoping to spread the blaze and make their escape. Outside the prison gate another crowd, friends and relatives of some of the prisoners, was trying to storm its way into the prison in the wake of the firemen. The firemen were helpless: they could find no way of approaching the fire. They had to be withdrawn while prison guards, armed with rifles and tear gas, beat back the rioters and cleared a way for them.

When the fire was out the bodies of 320 prisoners, many of them burned beyond recognition, were laid out in a large cattle shed to await burial.

What is one to say about a horrible affair like this? Surely, of all places, a prison, where thousands of men are locked up, should have every modern precaution against the spread of fire.

Those who were killed were criminals, sentenced by the state to terms of imprisonment. When they were sentenced the state assumed the responsibility for their safe custody during their imprisonment. But they all received the same sentence. They were killed by the state in a state-owned firetrap.

THE GLEN THEATER FIRE, PAISLEY

December 31st, 1929

PAISLEY is a drab industrial town which almost merges with its huge, sprawling neighbor, Glasgow. People who live there are mostly manual workers and small shopkeepers. In spite of the population of ninety thousand there is not a single registered hotel in the town. Visitors are encouraged to stay elsewhere.

The Glen Theater was neither big nor imposing. On the afternoon of December 31st, 1929, it held a capacity audience of 750 children, between the ages of two and sixteen. In passing, one wonders why children of two were sent to the movies, unless it was to get rid of them for the afternoon. And who was supposed to be taking care of them?

The operator's box was near the main entrance to the theater. A 'western' had just been shown and was being removed from this box to the rewinding room, when a strip of film came into contact with an electric line.

A cloud of pungent smoke and fumes arose from the film. The cinema manager, acting very swiftly, picked up the film and threw it out of the building onto some open ground. There it smouldered for a time and then went out.

There was no fire.

But somebody in the audience shouted 'fire,' and with smoke still blowing into the theater through the main entrance, a wild panic started among the children inside. In a terrified, screaming horde they ran away from the main entrance towards a narrow entrance at the screen-end of the theater. The manager, and a few adults present, shouting at the top of their voices, tried to persuade them to come back and use other exits, but their shouting went unnoticed. Many children, mad with fear, jumped from the theater balcony onto the heads of the children below.

Passers-by were horrified to hear a shrill, high-pitched screaming coming from the theater. There was still smoke drifting about the theater entrance: somebody put in a call to the fire department. When the firemen arrived they were told: 'Get smoke helmets. We can't get in through the smoke and the place is full of children.' The firemen went in without waiting for smoke helmets, and were joined by policemen.

But they were too late. In the words of one of the firemen: 'There was a solid mass of humanity around the screen when we fought our way in. Half-a-dozen terrified children grabbed my coat and belt, and I just turned and shoved them all out into the fresh air. Living and dead were piled breast high near the far exits. Some of the children were blue in the face: others could still scream.'

Flame-gutted wreckage of the Cocoanut Grove nightclub fire in Boston, in which 490 died

Flames consume the huge "big top" of the Ringling Brothers, Barnum & Bailey Circus in Hartford, Connecticut

Ambulances back up to the curb before the Hotel Winecoff in Atlanta, Georgia, in which 119 were killed by fire

Acme Photo

Bodies of more than a thousand passengers were recovered after the burning of the *General Slocum*, an excursion sidewheeler, in New York, 1904

A close-up view of the once proud luxury liner *Morro Castle*, beached and still smouldering at Atlantic City

Acme Photo

The German dirigible *Hindenburg*, caught in this remarkable photograph, falls in flames as it is being moored at Lakehurst, N. J.

A giant column of smoke rises above the shattered waterfront at Texas City, Texas, as an overheated oil storage tank explodes and burns

United Press Photo

General view of downtown Chicago after the fire of 1871

United Press Photo

Another fireman said: 'On the stairs leading to one exit the children were packed in a horrible heap. Behind the screen the space was packed with children, huddled together in every conceivable attitude. They were packed as tightly as a wall of cement bags. Some still moved: others were motionless.'

Policemen, firemen, and others worked to carry children out of the building, and every kind of conveyance was pressed into service to rush them to the hospital as quickly as possible. News of the tragedy had spread swiftly through Paisley, and hundreds of parents, who knew their children had been at the movies, besieged the theater and hospital, clamoring for news, thus greatly impeding the work of the doctors and nurses. One man learned that all three of his children were dead.

In this horror seventy children were killed and many others injured. A greater degree of competent adult supervision would have prevented the tragedy.

THE S.S. *NORMANDIE*

February 9th, 1942

THE *Normandie* (86,496 tons gross, over-all length 1027 feet) was the biggest ship in the world. She was the finest and costliest passenger ship ($60,000,000) ever build in a French shipyard. Some competent judges consider that she was the finest ship ever built in any shipyard. She was one of the most beautiful ships that ever crossed the Atlantic. With her sleek greyhound lines, her whaleback forecastle and protective breakwater above clipper bows, her tapering funnels and upper works, and the complete absence of winches and ventilators from her promenade decks, she made her chief rival, the *Queen Mary* (80,772 tons gross, over-all length 1018 feet) look a little stodgy by comparison.

Her interior was luxurious, matching her outside. In her magnificent saloons and staterooms were murals, wrought iron work, elaborate glass and sculpture, hand-woven carpets, and handmade furniture which represented the best in French art and craftsmanship. Her promenades were as wide as city streets; her shops, her restaurants and dining rooms were equal to anything which could be found in Paris. Her four screws, driven by turbo-alternators developing a thrust of 160,000 shaft horse power, gave her a top speed of over 30 knots. She carried a crew of 1,345 officers and men, and had accommodations for 2,170 passengers.

Her fire-fighting equipment was completely up to date. There were fire detectors in every cabin and stateroom, a sprinkler system throughout the whole ship, and automatic devices to cut off ventilation from any fire, thus restricting it to a small area. The ship's fire company had all received special training from the Paris fire department.

She was launched at St. Nazaire in October, 1932, and in the spring of 1935, her sea going trials completed satisfactorily, she was ready for her first Atlantic crossing. Her maiden voyage was a great occasion. Among her passengers was Madame Lebrun, wife of the French President, paying the first visit ever made by the wife of a French President to the United States.

The eyes of the world were upon her, and she fully lived up to the expectations of her builders, and of the whole French nation. On June 3rd, 1935, she entered New York harbor after a record breaking run of 4 days 11 hours 33 minutes (average speed 29.68 knots), and was given a tumultuous welcome. Tugs hooted, sirens screamed, and huge crowds lining the dockside cheered and waved as the ship, with immense dignity, steamed slowly up the Hudson and was maneuvered into her berth.

It was her hour of glory. She was the most celebrated ship in the world.

In August, 1939, the *Normandie* entered New York harbor for the last time. When war came the French, anxious for the safety of their best ship, would not allow her to sail again. She stayed in New York, with a skeleton crew aboard.

On May 15th, 1941, the United States Coast Guard placed a protective guard on the ship to prevent sabotage, and on December 12th, the Navy Department took the ship over, promising fair compensation to the owners. The intention was to convert her from a luxury liner into a troopship: authorities estimated that the equivalent of 2,400 large moving vans would be needed to remove the furniture and decorations which adorned her interior, and her huge stock of vintage wines.

She was renamed the *Lafayette*. This name was not unknown in French shipping circles. On May 5th, 1938, the French luxury liner *Lafayette* had been destroyed by fire while in dry dock in Le Havre. The fire had been caused by a man using an acetylene torch.

In February, 1942, the war news was not good. Luzon and Bataan were under attack, and would shortly fall. Singapore was on the point of falling. Rommel was attacking in Egypt. And all over the oceans of the world enemy submarines were taking enormous toll of Allied shipping. Every ton of shipping available was urgently needed for transporting troops and munitions. Many famous ocean liners, including the *Queen Mary*, already had been turned into troop transports. But still there were not enough. In that pressing hour there were two reasons why the swift recommissioning of the *Normandie* was of vital importance to the war effort. Her huge bulk would enable her to transport ten thousand troops on each trip, while her great speed rendered her fairly safe from anything except a very lucky submarine attack.

In peacetime the job of converting a passenger ship into a troop transport would almost certainly have been done in a dry dock. There was no time for that. The orders were that the *Normandie* should be made ready for sea in the shortest possible time.

By early February the job was almost completed, though work was still going on at top speed. Vast quantities of stores had been rushed to the dock and dumped in saloons and staterooms, ready to be stowed; part of the new crew had been signed on; it was hoped that in a few days the ship would be ready for sea. At two o'clock on the afternoon of February 9th there were 2,200 men aboard the ship—400 seamen, 300 coastguardmen, and 1,500 workmen.

The main saloon was stacked high with burlap-covered bales containing newly painted kapok life preservers wrapped in tar paper. In this saloon workmen with acetylene blowtorches were cutting through four steel stanchions which had formerly supported the decorations. On three of these stanchions the cutting had been completed.

A spark jumped. A small red glow appeared in the burlap covering one of the bales and flickered up into a flame. A man shouted: he and another man sprang at the bale, trying to beat out the flame with their bare hands. They were severely burned as the flame spread rapidly among the closely packed and highly flammable bales. In a few moments the fire was out of control.

A workman said: 'About thirty or forty men were working in the room. A spark from a blowtorch hit one of the bales and the fire began. We yelled for the fire watch, and Leroy Rosa and I tried to beat out the fire with our hands. Rosa's clothes caught fire, and I carried him out. The smoke and heat were terrific.'

The flames surged out of the saloon and spread with horrifying rapidity through the great superstructure of the ship. Almost without warning, workmen found themselves plunged into thick, sooty darkness, in which they choked and groped, yelling frantically to each other to ask what was happening.

Electricity supplies failed almost at once. And the up-to-date fire fighting installation left on the ship by the French was out of action. During the change-over it had been disconnected, and nothing, as yet, had been installed to replace it. New sprinklers were actually being fitted when the fire broke out, but they were not yet ready. Added to this, the ship had been filled with flammable material. There was nothing to stop the fire from spreading.

At 2:49, when the first fire alarm was turned in, men were already pouring in a confused, jostling crowd from the ship to the pier. Some made their getaway by swinging out a lifeboat and lowering it into the ice-encrusted water of the harbor.

A long procession of fire engines and ambulances came shrieking and clanging up to the pier, and police and firemen entered the ship to search for any workmen who might have been overcome by smoke. Many reached safety by an 85-foot extension ladder, rigged by the firemen to stretch from the roadway at the end of the slip to the sharp bows of the ship above.

From everywhere fire engines and fireboats were converging on the burning ship. A total of 24 engines, six hook and ladder companies, three fireboats, a water tower, a rescue squad, a searchlight squad, and a gas and water tender all took part in fighting the blaze. Within a few minutes of the first alarm being sounded, powerful jets were playing on the burning liner from all directions.

At first the efforts of the fire fighters seemed likely to have swift success. Licking flames, visible through the smoke haze, flickered, sank down, and disappeared. But hopes that the fire would be brought quickly under control were doomed to disappointment. Ninety minutes after the first outbreak a sudden burst of intense flame could be seen enveloping the captain's quarters under the bridge, and huge clouds of smoke began to belch from the entire superstructure. This smoke, pungent with the acrid smell of burning paint, was visible for miles around. It drifted in thick clouds into midtown Manhattan, and spread far into Brooklyn, Queens, and Nassau County. On Fifth Avenue the sun was only visible as a dull red ball: the area around the docks was in almost total darkness. On the New Jersey shore, where the wind kept the smoke away, thousands of people had gathered to watch the fire.

Medical and ambulance units from all parts of the city arrived on the scene, and doctors and nurses, coughing and choking in the thick smoke, treated cases as best they could. The badly burned cases were rushed to the hospital; those slightly injured, or merely suffering from smoke, were treated on the spot. Fire wardens, with their red and white armbands, worked with veteran firemen; sailors, most of them in their regulation blue but many in dungarees, hastily summoned from duty elsewhere, also came to help in the fight. An emergency hospital with one hundred cots was set up in the dock area, where more than two hundred firemen, suffering from the effects of smoke, were treated. Two mobile kitchens, also brought to the area, provided food and hot drinks for policemen, workers, and firemen.

For six hours the desperate fight went on, until, at about eight in the evening, the fire was brought under control. But then a new danger developed. Because of the thousands of tons of water pumped into her, the *Normandie* developed a twenty-one degree list to port. To counteract this, the Navy bored holes in her, and pumped more water into empty water tanks on her starboard side. For a time this succeeded in righting her, and at ten o'clock that night optimistic messages were issued by the authorities. The damage to the vessel, though severe, was chiefly confined to her superstructure: her engine room and other vital parts were hardly affected. There would be a delay, but not a very long one before she could be repaired and made ready to go to sea.

These hopes were not to be fulfilled. At 2.45 that night the strong incoming tide caused the big ship to topple, snapping the hawsers which secured her to the dockside. Quite gently, and with a prolonged crunching sound as her huge sides crushed through the ice, she heeled over and sank on her side in the slip. There she lay, her funnels just visible above the ice-covered water, with two of her four twenty-three-ton screws sticking grotesquely above the surface.

As soon as the story of the fire became known, the word 'sabotage' spread quickly from lip to lip. The sabotage theory received some support from the German radio, which claimed that the burning of the *Normandie* was a master stroke of one of their secret agents. There was no evidence whatever to confirm this claim, but much to contradict it. This was made clear in a statement issued by District Attorney Frank Hogan, who said: 'My office has conducted an extensive investigation of the fire on the *Normandie*. Approximately seventy witnesses have been examined. They were questioned by twenty assistant district attorneys . . .

'Witnesses are in substantial agreement as to the cause of the fire. An acetylene torch was being used to cut through four steel stanchions in the main saloon. Three had been cut through. The fourth was partially surrounded by a large number of burlap-covered bales said to contain life preservers.

'Alphonsus Gately, who was employed by the Robins Dry Dock and Repair Company, and who was in charge of operations, directed the removal of these bales. The testimony is that they were only moved two or three feet. Clement Derrick, of 925 Union Street, Brooklyn, who operated the burning torch, stated that his body, as he worked, touched the piles of bales . . .

'Flames were seen spreading from bale to bale with great rapidity. Twenty to twenty-five workmen attempted to stamp out the flames. The smoke and fire forced them out of the saloon. Gately backed up to the deck with the inactive fire hose, turned on the water, and directed the stream of water through the window at the burning bales. He testifies that the pressure was such that the stream only carried ten feet.'

The District Attorney ended his statement with these words:

'*The salient fact is that a flame causing sparks to fly was used within two or three feet of inflammable material. There is no evidence of sabotage. Carelessness has served the enemy with equal effectiveness.*'

One consoling feature is that casualties in this great fire were comparatively light. One man died: between two and three hundred others received treatment for injuries.

But the story of the *Normandie* was not quite ended. There was another chapter to come. After much consideration, naval authorities bravely decided to try to refloat her. They had no illusions about the magnitude of this task. They knew it would be the largest salvage job ever undertaken, that it might take two years to complete, and that the cost would run into millions. They thought it was worth trying. The contract was given to the Merritt Chapman and Scott Corporation, the best-known marine salvage company in the world.

Almost immediately a slight hitch occurred. On April 19th, while workmen were taking stores out of the side of the ship above the water line, black smoke was seen pouring out of her. Another fire had started, and it took three fireboats and twenty fire fighting units three hours to put it out.

This second fire was started by a spark from a welder's torch falling among flammable stores which workmen were taking out of the ship. After this a water main and fire hoses were installed along the whole length of the wreck and a twenty-four-hour fire watch was instituted under the command of officers from the New York City Fire Department. An order was issued that every man using a welding torch or acetylene cutter was to be accompanied by another man carrying a fire extinguisher.

The salvage company was faced by problems that were colossal. The size and weight of the ship posed questions of strain and stress which had never been calculated before. It will be remembered that the *Normandie* was lying on her side, and that to move her would mean subjecting every part of her to strains which had not been included by the shipbuilders in their original design. There was the danger that whole portions of the ship might cave inward suddenly if she were moved without due precautions being taken.

It was known that she rested partly on soft mud, and

partly on a rock ledge, but no one knew how much damage had been sustained by her submerged portion. This had to be ascertained by divers, who first had to repair the damage before the water could be pumped out of her so that she could be refloated. Never before had divers had such an arduous task.

All the ship's stores had tumbled together in vast, jumbled confusion against the side which rested on the river bottom. The ship was a maze of passages and staterooms. These passages had been easy enough to traverse in daylight, with the ship on an even keel. But, with the ship on her side, passages which had been eight feet high and four feet wide, had become four feet high and eight feet wide, and every doorway was a mantrap into which divers might sink unexpectedly. The mud in the water rendered divers' lights useless: everything had to be done by touch, in the dark. And the stores which littered the ship's bottom contained thousands of fragments of broken glass and jagged metal capable of cutting a life line.

Through open portholes, and holes in the ship's side, thousands of tons of soft river mud had entered. All this had to be taken out before the holes in the ship's side could be closed up; but as fast as it was removed it seemed to ooze in again. As a final difficulty, two of the city's sewers were discharged into the river near the wreck, and it became necessary to institute daily gas checks to guard against workers being poisoned by hydrogen sulphide gas.

In conditions of incredible difficulty, seventy skilled divers worked for months, closing portholes, sealing cracks, repairing holes in the ship's side. The deck had to be made watertight, and huge patches had to be fixed over the hatchways. The largest of these patches was fifty feet long and more than twenty feet wide. Working under water, divers had to construct bulkheads to strengthen those parts of the ship which would take the greatest strain when it moved. The entire interior of the ship was divided into fourteen separate watertight compartments.

At last, after months of painstaking calculation and effort, the work of pumping began. On September 13th, 1943, as the tide reached its flood, the great bulk of the ship, inert on the river bed for seventeen months, like a giant awakening, stirred slightly, and then, very slowly rolled upwards onto a moderately even keel. For the last time in her history the *Normandie* was saluted by the screaming of tugs' sirens and the cheering of spectators.

The world's biggest salvage job had been done successfully, and the world's biggest ship was afloat again. It had cost $4,750,000 to refloat her.

It would be pleasant to be able to record that the *Normandie* made many more successful voyages, but unfortunately this did not happen. She made only one more voyage, when she was towed out of the harbor to be broken up for scrap.

EXPLOSION IN A SCHOOL BUILDING, NEW LONDON, TEXAS

March 18th, 1937

THE world today runs largely on oil: the search for new oilfields goes on all the time. In many instances the discovery of oil has turned poor men into millionaires almost overnight, and has transformed sparsely populated rural districts into thriving communities within a few months. But there are risks attached to living in oil-bearing regions—the risks of fires, and explosions. The inhabitants of these regions are accustomed to such risks. Sometimes they grow careless about them.

New London, Texas, is situated in a district enriched by great reservoirs of natural oil. An estimate made in 1937 gave the number of oil derricks visible from the roof of the local school building as ten thousand. Seven derricks were actually within the school grounds.

Money from oil had built the school, and equipped it handsomely. In its spacious class rooms, gymnasium, and laboratories, a staff of about fifty teachers instructed fifteen hundred pupils from the surrounding district.

During the winter the class rooms were warmed by gas-heated steam radiators. At first the gas used was ordinary household gas. But in January 1937 a new system was tried out. The supply of ordinary gas was replaced by 'natural' gas, obtained by tapping a pipe line carrying waste gas away from the plant belonging to the Parade Oil Company. The great advantage in the use of this gas was that it cost nothing. In using it the school board was able to cut down the heating bill by $300 a month.

At 3 o'clock on the afternoon of March 18th, 1937, some of the primary school children had already gone home. In the manual training room, on the first floor, an instructor was giving a shop lesson to a class of boys. A girl named Martha Harris, who was working in the home economics building, some way from the main building, was looking out of the window. A little farther away, in the gymnasium, about a hundred mothers were attending a meeting of the Parent-Teachers Association.

In the manual training room, 16-year-old John Dow saw the instructor throw a switch to start one of the machines. Immediately below this switch was a trap door over a sub-basement, into which the natural gas was brought along pipes from the oilfield. John Dow saw the switch thrown, and then everything was blotted out in the roar of an explosion.

Martha Harris gave an account of what she saw from the window of the home economics building. 'I heard a roar. The earth shook, and brick and glass came showering down. I looked from the window, and saw my friends dying like flies. Children were blown out through the

111

top, on to the roof. Some of them hung up there, and others fell off, to the ground. I saw girls in my class jumping out of windows like they were deserting a burning ship.

'My brother said the place just blew up all of a sudden. It took his breath away, and all he knew was he had to jump somewhere, anywhere. I saw a girl fall out of the top down through a big window which opened to the outside. Glass cut her leg off just like a knife would.

'Children's bodies were stacked up like cakes after the explosion.'

Another witness said: 'There was a muffled sound and a rumble like distant thunder, and the walls bulged out. After a short, but perceptible interval, the roof rose suddenly up into the air, and crashed back again with a deafening roar, carrying most of the side walls with it. It all happened so quickly that there was no chance for escape or immediate rescue.'

Mothers, teachers, and more than a thousand riggers from the surrounding oilfields rushed to the scene and worked desperately to dig out survivors. Police and militiamen cordoned the wrecked building to prevent rescue work being impeded by frantic parents or morbidly curious sightseers. Mobile cranes were brought, and work continued all night by the light of arc lamps, and all through the following morning. Torrential rain soaked the rescuers and the anxiously waiting parents.

When all the 297 bodies had been brought out, the scene was pitiful in the extreme. A suggestion that the dead should be buried together in common graves was indignantly turned down by the grief-stricken parents. That afternoon, and all that night, embalmers were busy preparing bodies for interment. They worked in sheds, in fire stations, in mortuaries, with red-eyed, tired parents still wandering about seeking to identify their children. Many of the children were buried in the new suits and dresses which had been bought for them for Easter.

At a court of enquiry various witnesses gave evidence.

Mr. William Shaw, the School Superintendent (whose son was killed in the explosion) recalled that, a week earlier, he had directed a janitor to cut off an unused protruding gas pipe to below-floor level, and to recap it. He said that this might have been imperfectly done, and that gas might have leaked out and accumulated in hollow tiles under the floor. A spark could have set it off.

Mr. Shaw also said that the fuel used to heat the school radiators was 'natural' gas obtained by tapping the Parade Oil Company's waste gas line. He added that, while the Parade Company did not sell gas, it had not expressly forbidden him to tap its pipe line. 'They did not give me permission, but they were not averse,' he went on. The school board, he said, had approved the scheme for tapping the pipe line, thus eliminating the cost of fuel.

A member of the school board confirmed Mr. Shaw's statement, adding that several local churches had likewise tapped the Parade Company's line, and were getting fuel the same way.

A foreman of the Parade Company testified that it was his duty to search for lines tapping the pipe line, and to cut them off whenever he found them.

A heating engineer, whose bid for the installation of a hot water system in the school had been turned down, gave evidence that he had warned the school authorities that it was 'a crime to install a gas-steam system in a public building for which the system was not suited.'

An official of the United Gas Company stated that he had warned the board of the danger of using 'natural' gas. Other witnesses said that no inspection of the plumbing and heating system had been made when the school was built, that the school authorities had been warned that their gas regulator was inefficient and dangerous, that gas vents had not been examined regularly, and that gas pressure in the whole system had been excessively high.

This was a horrible tragedy, and who was to blame? The last thing the school authorities wished was that anything harmful should happen to any of the pupils. They were proud of the school, and in using natural gas to warm it they were only doing what dozens of other people in the district were doing. But sheer carelessness—a lack of adequate precautions—cost the lives of 297 children and teachers and injured many others.

One of the rescue squads, working in the ruins, found a blackboard on which the hand of a dead child had written:

'Oil and natural gas are East Texas' greatest blessings. Without them this school would not be here and none of us would be doing our lessons.'

THE PESHTIGO FOREST FIRE

1871

WILDFIRE has been the enemy of man from time immemorial. In ancient days our low-browed and savage ancestors, clutching their great stone clubs, fled, shrieking wildly, before the searing monster which roared and crackled through their primeval forests. They regarded forest fires as manifestations of divine displeasure. Nowadays we are more apt to look on them as the results of carelessness: but the effects are still the same. The red enemy goes on killing and destroying.

It is a solemn thought that a carelessly flung down match or cigarette or an inadequately extinguished camp fire may cause a conflagration which will burn hundreds of thousands of acres of forest or grassland, kill many men and cattle, and do millions of dollars' worth of damage. But it goes on happening.

Weather is the chief factor in determining the degree of forest fire danger. In certain parts of the world the degree of fire danger is expressed in terms of figures which range from o, representing no danger, to 100, representing maximum danger. Thus, with vegetation green or wet, air temperature mild, air humid, and wind slight, the fire danger index figure would be between o and 15, representing no immediate danger. With vegetation dry, high temperature, and dry air conditions, the danger index figure would be 75-85, representing a high degree of fire danger.

The extreme figure of 100 is only reached on 'blow-up days,' which are rare, averaging not more than three or four in any fire season. Such days contain every element which is likely to increase fire risk—very dry vegetation, dry air, following a drought, temperature in excess of 90° F., and a strong wind blowing. In these conditions any tiny spark or ember is likely to cause a fire and the smallest fire is difficult to control, even in its earliest stages.

Forest and bush fires are usually classified in three groups:

Ground Fires. Fires burning in thick layers of humus and vegetable matter.

Surface Fires. Fires burning just above the ground in grass, low shrubs or fallen leaves.

Crown Fires. Fires burning in the top foliage of trees. There are two types of crown fires. (*a*) Running crown fires, which occur when the fire in the crowns of trees progresses ahead of the main surface fires. (*b*) Dependent crown fires, which are fires in the top branches of trees sustained by heat and flames from the surface fire below.

There are also 'spot' fires. These are the result of sparks or burning fragments from the main fire being projected ahead to form entirely new fires in other places. In very bad conditions spot fires may break out five or six miles away from a main fire.

Fire-fighting in heavily timbered and mountainous country requires special techniques, and the fire-fighting organization in the huge wooded areas of America has a resemblance to the chain of command in a large army. Watch towers, eighty to ninety feet high and provided with two-way radio and telephone communication, are placed in strategic positions and manned whenever the temperature is high and humidity low. From these towers reports are sent to district posts, from district posts to area headquarters, from area headquarters to command headquarters, where situation maps depict the fire situation over huge tracts of country. Fire fighting commands have their own meteorological services, their own spotting aircraft and, in some instances, they employ 'paratroop' fire fighters, who can be dropped into lonely and inaccessible places where a dangerous fire is developing. When big fires are burning, thousands of men may be employed to fight them. These men may have to be moved rapidly from one place to another to contain and repulse new fires. As in all fire or military operations, speed, and the application of maximum force at the critical point, are of the highest importance. A small fire, left for only a few minutes, can easily develop into a huge conflagration blazing out of control on a forty-mile front.

On level ground, in still air, fires tend to spread out-wards in all directions, assuming a circular shape.

In very bad conditions, in dense, heavy grass, or up steep hills, with a strong following wind, the rate of advance of a fire may be greatly accelerated. A rate of advance of up to twenty miles an hour is not uncommon.

A fire burning in wild, and possibly mountainous country, with no roads leading to it, and no water supplies readily available, cannot be fought with the methods used in fighting a fire in a built-up district with a hydrant on every corner. Forest and bush fires are not 'put out.' They have to be stopped, and the only way to stop them is by clearing an area in front of them in which there is nothing left for them to burn. This cleared area, which obviously will have to vary in width according to the size and fierceness of the fire, is known as the control line. The tools used by firemen for clearing the fire line consist of various forms of shovels, rakes, and axes specially designed and constructed for the purpose. Bull-dozers, ploughs and tractors are also often employed to help in clearing a line in front of an advancing fire.

But the behavior of a fire is not predictable. Picture to yourself an enormous fire, swallowing up hundreds of trees in its forward progress, advancing on a two-mile front with a fifteen-mile-an-hour wind behind it. Ahead of the fire hundreds of men are working to construct a line, entirely cleared of flammable material, and wide enough to stop the fire. Many more men are engaged in extinguishing spot fires, caused by flying sparks and embers from the main conflagration. If not extinguished at once, any of these spot forces may start another conflagration.

Imagine the smoke, the heat, the tired, aching muscles, the anxiety: 'Will the line hold?'

And then, with a sudden change of wind, the fire roars away in an entirely different direction. New spot fires start in places where there are no fire-fighters available to deal with them. Within a few minutes an entirely different and untouched section of the forest may become a raging furnace.

Another method of fighting forest fires is called 'backfiring.' This may be very effective: occasionally it is the only method of fighting a big fire. But it can also be very dangerous, and should be used only by experts. When used by inexperienced fire-fighters it may only increase the fire, or create fresh fires.

Backfiring, or burning back, consists of lighting another fire ahead of the main fire.

Hot air rises. There is in a fire, a constant stream of hot air going upwards, while cooler air is being drawn in at the base of the fire to replace it. For this reason, whatever the direction of the main air stream, the wind in the immediate vicinity of any fire is always blowing towards the fire.

The trick in backfiring is to take advantage of this suction, and light the forward fire at just the right moment for the flames from it to be drawn towards the main blaze. The effect of this is to create two fires, some distance apart, each advancing towards the other. When they meet a strip of ground will have been burned off in front of the main fire, so creating a fire line of ground which has already been burned over. If this line can be made wide enough, it will contain the fire and halt its forward progress.

On the night of October 8th, 1871, two fires broke out which must rank among the greatest and most tragic in the history of the world. One was the great fire of Chicago, which burned down seventeen thousand buildings and killed 250 people. (See page 163.) The other, the worst forest fire in the history of the United States, devastated enormous tracts of country in Wisconsin and Michigan, and killed 1,500 people.

For fourteen weeks there had been a severe drought. In the woods of Michigan and Wisconsin streams and springs were dried up in many sections, and water, for family use, and for cattle, had become a luxury, and an expensive one. The woods were hazy with the smoke of many forest fires, but until October 8th, these fires seemed to be fairly well under control. Then came a gale from the south-west, and with tragic suddenness many small fires joined together to form a conflagration of stupendous size. Some idea of the sheer size of the fire can be obtained from a description by a newspaper correspondent, who saw it from the safety of a passenger boat on one of the lakes. He wrote:

The fire on the east side of the Bay extended in an almost unbroken line from the eastern shore of Lake

Winnebago to the northern extremity of the Eastern Pen-
insula, a distance of 150 miles. So deep and dismal was the
darkness caused by the immense volume of smoke that
the sun was totally obscured for a distance of two hun-
dred miles. The boat left Escanaba for Green Bay on the
fatal Sunday night at twelve o'clock, but only made her
way twelve miles out when forced to return by the
stormy sea beneath and the sea of fire overhead. The air
was red with burning fragments carried from Peshtigo
and other places along the shore, a distance of fifty miles.

Peshtigo is a name of tragic memories. Once it was a
thriving small town, built by William B. Ogden, of Chicago, to 'make money for its founder and keep up the
lumber interests.'

The town was built in a clearing on both sides of the
Peshtigo River, on a site 'well chosen for beauty as well
as for business.' The works of the Peshtigo Company
were situated on the north-eastern bank of the river:
other business establishments and residential quarters were
on the south-western bank. The streets were well laid
out, the houses 'prettily built and carefully painted,' and
'little ornamental gardens were frequent.' Roads cut
through the forest communicated with prospering ham-
lets and thriving farms to the west and south, and a railroad connected the little city with the Great Lakes. The
population in 1871 was between two and three thousand.

During the drought of that autumn of 1871 there had
been many fires in the surrounding woods: some of them

had penetrated almost to the outskirts of the town. Some of them were still smouldering, in dried furze and brown herbage, deep in the woods.

But nobody was greatly uneasy. Every precaution had been taken. A cleared strip all the way round the town provided an adequate fire line, and it was known that the first rain to fall in the forest would quench the fires still smouldering there.

No rain came. On Sunday evening, October 8th, a violent gale sprang up suddenly, sweeping through the forests from the south-west.

That Sunday [wrote a reporter] *was noticed as a chilly day, though the atmosphere was still and filled with smoke. The smoke created no alarm, as the smouldering fires in the pineries about sufficiently accounted for it. Towards evening the smoke increased while the chilliness in the atmosphere perceptibly abated and early in the evening gave way to occasional hot puffs from the burnt districts.*

Sunday evening, after church, the town was quiet; the smoke from the fires in the region had become so thick as to be stifling and hung like a funeral pall over everything.

Soon after eight in the evening, with the warmth of the atmosphere increasing and the smoke almost suffocating in its intensity, a sullen rumbling began to be heard far away in the south-west. At half-past eight the far-off rumbling had increased to a steady roar, like distant thunder or the coming of heavy freight trains at full speed. Men felt their way through the smoky streets and congre-

122

gated at the hotels and other places of resort, and discussed the strange sounds. Anxious mothers nervously and hesitatingly put their little ones to bed, and then peered out in the dismal streets to see what they could see.

Nine o'clock came, and with it an alarming increase of the unknown sound, which now resembled the roar of a dozen freight trains at full speed.

Suddenly there was a cry of fire sounding through the smoke-beclouded streets, and men rushed hither and thither through the impenetrable blackness, rubbing their eyes for sight, and stumbling against each other as they ran. But no fire was found, though the search extended out of the village and into the edge of the woods.

Scarcely had the first alarm subsided when the cry was raised again, in another quarter, and the blind running and stumbling was renewed. While this confusion was at its height, and while most of the men were away from their houses, angry puffs of almost burning heat came sweeping through the town while, at quick intervals, a frightful glare penetrated the smoke from the south-west.

Mothers caught their children from their beds and hastily dressed them. A cry of terror filled the town. Men, women and children, horses, dogs, oxen, swine, fowl— everything that had life ran wildly to escape the impending destruction.

Then, with the howling of a tornado came a storm of fire which rained down on the doomed village like flaming missiles shot from unseen artillery. The heavens rained fire on every hand as if to consume the whole earth.

Houses crumpled like paper, and flaring roofs were

123

borne away like gigantic sparks upon the fiery gale. People threw themselves on the ground and perished where they fell. The storm of falling cinders was followed quickly by a continuous blaze that licked up everything with which it came in contact.

Some, who had sought refuge in the river, saved themselves by keeping their bodies submerged, only raising their heads at intervals to gasp for breath. Many were drowned in the effort to escape burning, while others, who sought to catch breath, inhaled livid flame, and perished. Even the fishes were reached by some mysterious agency, so that the next day hundreds of them were found floating dead.

That was how the big fire came to Peshtigo. Seven hundred and fifty were dead in the small town. Morning found hundreds of survivors, many of them badly burned, wet through and miserable, still crouching in the water of the river. Where the village had been was a blackened ruin with not a house standing: the ground was too hot to walk on. Later that day a railroad gang, led by an ex-prize fighter named Mulligan, forced a way across miles of burning prairie and blockaded roads and brought supplies and help.

Peshtigo suffered the worst blaze, but in other places fires were almost equally severe. White Rock, Forestville, Elm Creek, Huron City, Seigal, Bingham—the list of burned villages goes on and on. And many isolated farms were burned and their owners perished.

A farmer named James Langworth lived near St.

Charles, Saginaw County, on a farm of ninety acres. On the Sunday of the big fire he was alone on the farm, his wife and children being on a visit to friends in Canada.

His well had been dry for a week: his only source of water supply during that time had been what he could get by digging holes in the dry bed of a stream. During the day about a barrel of water would collect in these holes. This he used for drinking and cooking purposes.

On the Sunday morning of the fire clouds of smoke were drifting across the farm, making everything dark. The farmer had a cow and several head of young stock on the farm. These seemed to be suffering so terribly from the effects of the smoke that that Sunday afternoon he turned them loose. They started away in the direction of the village, and he never saw them again.

At that time, Sunday afternoon, he reckoned that forest fires were burning a mile away from him, but were not heading in the direction of the farm. Between the farm and the edge of the forest was a partially dried-up swamp, nearly half a mile wide. If the fires did turn in his direction, he was confident that the swamp would stop them. He was worried, but not frightened.

Shortly before dark his farm was suddenly invaded by hundreds of wild animals—rabbits, woodchucks, squirrels, moving slowly, as if dazed, over his land. When he approached them they took no notice of him.

That night the farmer sat up in his farmhouse, his oil-lamp a dim blur in the smoke-filled room. Soon after midnight the wind changed and freshened, and in the distance he could hear the roar of the flames, and the crash-

125

ing of big trees as they toppled over. At six o'clock in the morning there was no daylight—only thick smoke billowing, and the roar of the flames becoming steadily louder. He could not see the fire, but from the sound of the flames he judged that it must have eaten its way around the edges of the swamp and was approaching the farmhouse. He decided to leave.

He made a pile of a few valuables on top of a blanket, and tied up the blanket. As he was tying it, huge flames suddenly shot up from his barns and haystacks, and a rain of burning twigs and branches swept in through the open doorway of the farmhouse. James Langworth abandoned his bundle, and ran for his life.

There was a wagon road from his farm to the village, and he sought this as a means of escape. Almost stifled, his throat so parched that he could not swallow, and his lungs feeling as if a knife was at work in them, he stumbled forward, trying to keep ahead of the fire. And then another fire, coming from a different direction, jumped the road in front of him.

Behind him was the main fire, to the right was another sheet of flames, and trees ahead of him were burning. He turned to the left, which was still clear, though burning cinders were falling, and small flames were already jumping up in the dry leaves which covered the ground. Several times, covering his face with his arms, he had to run in a series of leaps through small surface fires.

Twisting and turning, falling into holes, stumbling over logs, he staggered on, not knowing where he was going. And at last, with his clothes almost scorched off him, and 'covered with blisters,' he ran into a gang of men working in the smoke to construct a fire-line around the village of St. Charles.

James Langworth lost everything he had in the fire, except his life and his family who were away. He was among the lucky ones.

Terrible tragedies occurred on outlying and lonely farms. When the fire was approaching, the Lamp family, consisting of Charles Lamp, his wife and five children, hitched up a wagon and tried to escape with some of their household goods. The fire caught up with them, and all were killed except Charles Lamp, who was horribly burned. A farmer named Lawrence, with his wife and four children, tried to take refuge in a large clearing: all were burned. Two substantial farmers, Nathaniel May and Henry Newberry, were neighbors. Mr. May's family consisted of himself, his wife, and his daughter. At the time of the fire they had friends from New York staying with them—a Mr. and Mrs. William Aldous, with their three children.

The Newberry family farmed, between them, about a thousand acres and owned a mill. Different members of the family owned their own houses. One of them, a Mr. William Newberry, was a school-teacher.

On the night of the fire this Mr. William Newberry heard a 'great roaring,' and found that fire was raging in the woods not far away. He started to go to his brother's house to see what must be done, but was driven back by suffocating smoke. On his return he found that his house was alight.

He, his wife, their child, and his wife's sister all fled blindly into the smoke. By the greatest good luck they came to a small water hole, twelve feet square. There they squatted, covering themselves with water, their backs to the fire. Soon the fire was raging on all sides of them: they saw the Mays' barn and a bridge spanning a dry creek go up in flames within a few seconds, and they could hear shouting and screaming from the Mays' house.

They survived. In the morning, half-blinded, they staggered out of the water hole, and Mr. Newberry went to look for his relatives. A short distance from the water hole he found the bodies of two men, and, farther on, the carcasses of several hogs and cows. Finding he was too blind to go on, he cut some meat from one of the dead cows and took it back to his family, who cooked and ate it.

Of the Newberry family twelve out of seventeen were killed. All the May family and their guests were killed. On another farm belonging to a man named Adnah Newton, sixteen persons were burned to death. On other farms the Doyle family, a husband and wife and seven children, the Hill family, of ten persons, the Spear family, a husband and wife and two children, all perished.

A Mr. Brady of Detroit was staying in the village of White Rock, Huron County, on that Sunday night. As the fire approached the village, the villagers turned out to try to fight it. Finding this hopeless, they 'fled into the waters of the Great Lake, and even here were not safe from the scorching air without occasional plunges beneath the surface.'

Mr. Brady himself was in the water for eight hours. About him were 'men up to their waists or shoulders in water, holding children in their arms, and women but poorly protected by their clothing from the chill of the water which was their only protection against the burning heat of the air.' Huddled in the water, half-blinded by smoke and heat, they saw the fire eat up the whole of their village. In Mr. Brady's words: 'Not only were their houses, fences, barns and stock destroyed, but their furniture and clothing, and even the deeds by which they held their lands, and their insurance papers."

On the Monday morning, when the fires had passed by, the exhausted villagers crawled out of the water, but 'there was neither food nor shelter for miles around.'

Later in the afternoon they were taken aboard the lake steamer *Huron*, which also took the rescued inhabitants of Forestville and Cato, who were in a similar plight.

Near Gardner, Wisconsin, three brothers named Williamson owned a sawmill and lumber business which employed the entire population of a small hamlet situated in a clearing in the forest. There were four buildings in this clearing—the mill, the storehouse, the general boarding-house, and a barn, and some seventy people lived in the settlement.

For weeks, during the drought, fires had been burning in the neighboring woods, and they had taken precautions to guard the settlement. A fire-line, nearly a mile wide, had been burned off all around the settlement, making what must have seemed an impregnable fire-stop.

It was not enough. When the gale hit the forest, sending hundred-feet-high flames roaring through the trees, a huge rain of burning fragments came down on the settlement. In a few minutes everything was in flames and wild panic broke out. According to survivors there was time for everyone to get away by taking to the woods in a direction away from the fire. Instead of doing this, many fought to take refuge in a well, and others struggled madly to gain possession of a small pit dug in a potato patch.

Sixty-one people were killed, including the whole of the Williamson family.

A family of French settlers named Méchand lived on a small farm in North Wisconsin. There were four in the family—Mr. and Mrs. Méchand, a son named Louis, aged six, and Mrs. Méchand's mother, who was a little mentally deficient.

On the morning of October 11th, while they were breakfasting, a neighbor came running into the house and told Mr. Méchand that he must come out immediately and see what could be done: the forest fires were coming uncomfortably close. Mr. Méchand took his time about finishing his breakfast, and went out.

Smoke began to drift across the farm. Mr. Méchand returned about noon, and Mrs. Méchand asked him if he thought there was any danger. He shook his head and answered, 'No.'

The family sat down to dinner. As they were finishing, another neighbor looked in and said that the fire was advancing at a 'frightful' speed. In Mrs. Méchand's words:

The air was stifling, and the smoke got into one's lungs and nostrils in such a way as to render it extremely unpleasant. Mother sat in a corner holding little Louis in her lap, and I noticed that she seemed restless and that her eyes shone with a wild light that I had only seen in the old days when she was about to have an outburst of fury.

I was frightened and fidgety and didn't do anything in the right way. I went and took the boy away from Mother, who relinquished him readily: and then, as I had afterwards terrible reason to remember, she went to the cupboard and secreted something in the bosom of her dress. Mr. Méchand stood at the door speaking hurriedly with the neighbor, when a burning branch of pine fell at his feet. Instantly the air darkened, a violent puff of wind rushed upon us, and smoke poured in volumes about the house. Then, following the gust, a bright wall of fire seemed to be pushing down almost on us, and everything was in flames.

Mr. Méchand cried out to me to bring Louis with me, and seized Mother by the hand, and we all four ran out in the woods ahead of us. I ran on, blinded and choked by the smoke, and carrying Louis in my arms. He was pale with terror and did not utter a single cry, but clung to my neck as I hurried on, stumbling and tripping at every step. I kept calling to my husband to keep in sight, but there was no need of doing so, for I could see that Mother was a great worry to him, and he had almost to drag her along. She kept looking from side to side and trying to break away from him.

The family ran for three miles, Mrs. Méchand carrying the six-year-old boy, Mr. Méchand dragging the grandmother. They outran the fire and paused, exhausted, in the smoke-filled woods, with the fire a good mile behind them. Mrs. Méchand put the boy down; her husband released the grandmother. For a few moments it was safe to take a rest.

Then the grandmother ran away.

Before they could stop her, she was lost amid the trees and smoke. Mr. Méchand ran after her and 'in the terror of the moment,' Mrs. Méchand ran after him, leaving the child.

After running for a minute or two, she suddenly realized that she was lost. She had no idea which direction she had taken, where the child was, where her husband was.

Madly I tried to retrace my steps but there was nothing to guide me—no path, no blazes on the trees. The wind shook the trees and almost bent them double: the sultry air filled with smoke, and all the horrors of my condition made me frantic. I rushed about helplessly crying and screaming, "Louis! Louis! Father!"

After a quarter of an hour's frantic searching Mrs. Méchand found her son, but not her husband or her mother. By this time the fire was getting close: 'among the treetops sparks and firebrands were whirling in the air.' They ran on, the woman still carrying the boy, till they came to a clearing, where they had to rest.

132

After dark they set out again, and were caught up in a stampede of wild animals. Mrs. Méchand's story goes on:

I heard a mingled gnashing and hoarse barking, which I instantly recognized as that of wolves, and I had scarcely time to snatch up Louis and run behind a tree before they rushed by me. They did not stop for an instant: and when they had passed there came in their track a herd of deer, uttering cries that seemed almost human in their intense agony. The stampede lasted a good ten minutes, and when it was over I saw the woods already burning and felt the terrible heat on my face.

I turned and fled in the wake of the deer and the wolves. My shoes were stripped from my feet and my ankles were torn and bloody. Finally I sank to the ground with the boy in my arms.

I know nothing of what passed then till I was rudely shaken by the shoulder and heard a wild gibbering laugh. I opened my eyes, and above me stood my mother with a drawn knife in her hand.

"Ho, ho," she screamed. "Fine time of night for a mother and child to be running through the woods. Look at the red light—it is the light of dawn. And the rocks are burning. Call upon them to fall on you. The Lord is coming, and the wheels of His chariot burn with His mighty driving. Let us go up to meet Him."

I sprang to my feet and cried: "Mother, what are you doing. Do you want to kill me and Louis?"

"Kill you! Yes. Why wait? The Lord calls and the devil drives. He has let loose his imps against the world. The

133

trees are falling in the forest: all hell's demons pull them down with hooks of fire. I will kill you: would you burn to death? Come, let us go," and she seized Louis, while the knife gleamed in her hand.

I sprang at her with all my strength and struggled with her. Torn, bleeding as I was, the thought of my child gave me strength. I overpowered the mad woman: I seized her throat and would have strangled her. Her insanity had almost made me mad.

But then, I thought, she was my mother, and my hand was stayed, and when she rose to her feet all her wildness was gone and in its place had returned that calmness, almost imbecility, which had characterized her for the last few years. She was ready and willing to do all I told her, but I kept the knife in my hand.

The woods were now not as intolerably hot: the wind had dropped, and a light rain was falling. We went on for an hour or two longer, and then lay down in a hollow and fell asleep. When we awoke men were around us who gave us food and shelter, and as soon as we were able we went to Green Bay. There I soon recovered from the sickness and terror of that dreadful night. My mother continues in the same state of imbecility, which the doctor says will soon become complete dementia. Louis was not long in recovering. I have heard nothing of my husband.

That is Mrs. Méchand's story.

One village successfully fought the fire. In Marinette, Mr. A. C. Brown, the senior partner in a large mill, turned out all his men and teams to form a line along a wide avenue which had been cut through the trees some time previously. For fourteen hours the teams hauled water, while the men drenched the ground and trees. The fire swept past the village and obliterated the neighboring village of Menekaune, burning down two large mills, the Catholic and Methodist Churches, the schoolhouse, and every house in the village.

Marinette became a hospital center. A correspondent visiting the village described what he saw.

The buildings are of rough boards, very similar to the barracks of the army. The first patient as you enter is an American, who has with him his wife, babe, and five other children. The fire approached them so rapidly that they had to run for their lives without saving anything except what they had on. They reached a small pool, where they sat for hours till the fury of the fire had passed when, terribly burned, they were brought to town to be cared for. The next patient, an old German, lost his wife, daughter, son and eight grandchildren. In another bed an old lady is dying, the only one left of a family of ten. The next three beds are occupied by the Hoyt family, or what is left of them, some half-a-dozen having perished. The next is a double bed occupied by two full-grown men, members of a Wisconsin regiment. One of them, Lovett Reed, started to run for a clearing, but, finding he could not reach it, took out his pocket-knife and tried to commit suicide by stabbing himself to the heart. After inflicting several severe, though not fatal wounds, he accidentally dropped his weapon and his design was frustrated. The

*fire passed over, leaving him only slightly burned and he
is now recovering.*

Others tried successfully to commit suicide when cut
off by the flames. One man killed his whole family, and
then committed suicide himself. A wealthy farmer shot all
his fine horses, and then died with them. Many of the
injured were blinded, some temporarily, others for life. A
peculiarity which was noticed by some observers was
that no Indian seems to have died in the fire. Possibly they
knew better how to take refuge from forest fires than the
white settlers.

All roads and telegraph communications had been cut
by the fires, and it was some days before the outside
world, already shocked by the immense tragedy of the
fire which burned Chicago, learned the full extent of the
simultaneous devastation in Michigan and Wisconsin. Peshtigo, White Rock, Forestville, Elm Creek, Huron City,
Bingham, Verona, Holland, Manistee—the names read like
a roll call. In an area of the peninsula between Saginaw
Bay and Lake Huron, twenty-three towns and villages
were burned out and eighteen partially destroyed. Hundreds of isolated farms were turned into blackened des-
erts. Millions of trees became charred stumps. Thousands
of animals died pathetically and miserably. Thousands of
people were left ruined and homeless. And more than
1,500 men, women and children lost their lives.

THE MAINE AND NEW HAMPSHIRE FOREST FIRES

1947

YEAR after year, whenever there are conditions of drought, fire sweeps through large areas of forest on the American continent. California, Montana, Idaho, New Brunswick, Oregon, Ontario, all have had their bad years. In Minnesota, in 1918, a huge forest fire killed more than five hundred people. This was the worst American forest fire since Peshtigo.

In 1947 it was the turn of Maine and New Hampshire. The month was October, and autumn leaves were falling. In the pine forests the pine-needles were lying thickly. Everything was bone-dry after a long drought. For twenty-three days no rain had fallen.

During three days, between October 20th and October 23rd, nine major fires broke out. All over the affected districts of Maine and New Hampshire were scenes of confusion as trucks carrying fire fighters and equipment, hurrying to the fires, met trucks and cars loaded with refugees seeking a place of safety.

One of these fires broke out near U.S. Highway 1, not far from the village of Kennebunk, Maine, on October

20th. It was almost certainly caused by human carelessness. In its early stages it jumped the highway, and moved
towards the village of Fortune Rock, on the Atlantic
coast.

Fire fighters were drawn from the surrounding country and help was sent by the U.S. Coastguard, which sent
fire-fighting trucks. The fire was fought with resolution.
Thousands of men manned the fire line, and bulldozers
were used to smash through timber and undergrowth,
creating firebreaks. But 'blow-up' conditions helped the
flames. Other fires, started by burning embers, joined with
the main fire to kindle a massive conflagration. Kennebunk had to be abandoned, and, on October 21st, the
flames swooped with dramatic suddenness on the villages
of Goose Neck and Cape Porpoise, destroying two hundred homes and the forty-room Belvidere Hotel.

The 23rd of October was disastrous. A sudden shift in
the thirty-mile-an-hour wind sent flames roaring down
on the village of Fortune Rock. So sudden was the onset
that before anything could be done they had spread from
one frame building to another, destroying 150 homes and
four hotels.

There were fires everywhere, over a vast tract of countryside. On this day, Octobet 23rd, Governor Horace
Hildreth declared a state of emergency, calling the disaster the worst in Maine's history. President Truman ordered the appropriate federal agencies to supply emergency relief.

Not far away an even larger fire was raging in York
County of New Hampshire. This fire started near the

small town of Newfield, and by the 21st it had burned out 126,000 acres and was menacing the town of Waterborough. It was only prevented from joining the Kennebunk fire by the broad Maine super-highway, which acted as a firebreak.

On the 23rd, while thousands of men were fighting these two big fires, another separate fire, started by embers carried by the wind, flared swiftly on a fifty-two-mile front, and destroyed three-quarters of the village of East Waterborough. In Newfield on the same day, the town hall and all the town records were burned. By the 24th, 160 square miles of country had been swept by this fire.

Yet another fire, swinging south, blazed through the villages of Brownfield Center and East Brownfield, destroying 175 homes. Yet another, driven from the Arcadia National Park by a wind of gale force, roared into the fashionable resort of Bar Harbor, driving the inhabitants and holiday-makers away. For a time the town was completely cut off, surrounded by a ring of fire. By heroic efforts the fire was held back from the main thoroughfare, but 272 homes on the outskirts of the town were destroyed.

For five days, like panzer divisions, great fires swept on remorselessly over huge tracts of countryside. Everywhere they attacked they were fought until finally, with the coming of rain, they were held and subdued. But the cost was heavy.

Millions of feet of timber had been burned, twelve hundred homes destroyed, six thousand people had been rendered homeless. Sixteen lives had been lost.

THE VICTORIA, AUSTRALIA, FOREST FIRE

1939

In January, 1939, in Melbourne, Australia, officials were watching the weather anxiously. During 1938 the rainfall recorded in Melbourne had totaled 17.63 inches for the year. This was five inches below the yearly average. All over the State of Victoria vegetation was dry.

January, 1939, came in with an increasing glare of heat. Throughout December many bush fires had been burning, because of the dryness of the vegetation, but these were regarded as 'under control.' Unless conditions worsened, the fire fighters had the situation in hand.

On January 6th Melbourne had a shade temperature of 75° F. with a relative humidity of fifty-nine per cent. On the 7th, the temperature rose to 82° F. with a humidity of forty-one per cent. And then, on January 8th, there came a 'blow-up' day with a shade temperature of 110° F., a relative humidity of seven per cent, and winds of up to forty miles an hour.

In a matter of hours smouldering fires joined together to form vast conflagrations. Towering flames jumped the fire lines and roared away out of control. Telegraph lines were cut, and motorists, racing to warn outlying mills and villages, were beaten to it by the flames.

On January 9th the temperature dropped to 76° F., and wearied fire fighters hoped that the end of the emergency was in sight. Then, on January 10th, the shade temperature in Melbourne rose to 112° F., an all-time record; in outlying districts temperatures of 119° F. were recorded.

Whole townships had to be evacuated: roads were crowded with blinded and hysterical refugees. Hospitals were filled with men and women suffering from fire blindness and burns. Manning the fire lines, the fire fighters struggled against hopeless odds. Burning bark, carried long distances, continually ignited fresh fires which, in turn, blazed into conflagrations. A pall of black smoke covered hundreds of miles of countryside, reducing visibility to a few yards. In a few hours the towns of Omeo, Warrendyte, Nooje, and Woodpoint ceased to exist.

In Melbourne, the state capital, the wind was described as being 'like a breath from a furnace'; many people died from heat-stroke. Smoke from the burning bush enveloped the town in a dusky twilight. Water began to run low, owing to the destruction of watersheds, and restrictions had to be imposed.

On Thursday, January 12th, the temperature dropped to 78° F., and again it was hoped that the worst was over. This hope was not realized.

On Friday, January 13th, the shade temperature in Melbourne rose abruptly to a new all-time record of 114° F.

141

In a description of the period given by Judge L. E. B. Stretton, he wrote: 'On that day it appeared that the whole state was alight.'

Matlock, Rubicon, Narbethong, Tangil, Colac, Toolangi, Grampians, Aberfeldie, Hillend . . . the number of villages swept by fire, many of them with fatal casualties, went on mounting. In Judge Stretton's words:

Townships were obliterated in a few minutes. Mills, houses, bridges, tramways, machinery, were burned to the ground: men, cattle, horses, sheep, were devoured by the fire or asphyxiated by the debilitated, scorching air.

Steel girders and machinery were twisted by heat as if they had been of fine wire. Sleepers of heavy durable timber set in soil, their upper surfaces flush with the ground, were burnt through. . . . Houses of brick were seen and heard to burst into a roar of flames before the fires had reached them. Great pieces of flaming bark were carried by the wind to set in raging flame regions not yet reached by the fire. Such was the force of the wind that in many places hundreds of trees of great size were blown clear of the earth with tons of soil and embedded masses of rock still adhering to the roots: for mile upon mile the former forest monarchs were laid in confusion, burnt, torn from the earth, and piled one upon another as matches strewn by a giant hand.

Many people had to escape from the fire three or four times. Having reached a point which they considered a place of safety, they found, before many hours, that the

142

fire was rushing on them again. One family of six, escaping in an automobile, missed a turn in the smoke, and crashed into the fire. The two parents gathered their four children together, placed them in the road, and lay down on top of them. All were seriously burned, but all survived.

Casualties were heavy, though not on the scale of the Peshtigo fire. The worst single episode was at Matlock, where a rescue party, after spending hours climbing over thousands of burned trees, found fifteen men dead in the sawdust pit of a mill.

In all, seventy-one people were killed in these fires: many others were injured. Millions of acres of forest were burned over, and the wild life in it obliterated. The amount of the damage done was incalculable.

IN the German elections of 1928, thirteen National Socialist (Nazi) candidates were elected to the Reichstag. Events were to swell this number considerably during the next five years.

Herr Stresemann, the German Chancellor, the leader of the moderate Social Democratic party, died in 1929. Three weeks after his death the big Wall Street crash heralded a huge economic slump, and unemployment figures began to rise everywhere. In the United States they rose to twelve million, in Great Britain to over three million. Germany had one million, three hundred thousand unemployed in 1929, three million in 1930, and nearly six million in 1932.

The German people, plunged into depression, were looking for somebody who would *do* something about the state of the country, and Adolf Hitler announced that he was the man.

The Nazis began to win votes. In the election of July, 1932, they won 230 seats out of 609. This number of seats, while not giving them an outright majority, made them the largest single party in the Reichstag. Field-Marshal Paul von Beckendorf and von Hindenburg, the aged President of Germany, offered Hitler the position of Vice-Chancellor, with Franz von Papen as Chancellor. Hitler declined the offer.

At that time a good deal of jockeying for power was going on in Germany between Franz von Papen and General Kurt von Schleicher. Each was intriguing against the other in order to be Chancellor: each was looking for allies in the various parties that then made up the Reichstag. The result was complete instability, a kind of see-saw in which each, in turn, pushed the other out.

Von Papen resigned, and an election was held in November, 1932. The results, to Hitler, were far from pleasing. His party lost more than two million votes, and thirty-four seats. But, with 196 members elected, they were still the strongest single party in the House.

Von Schleicher took office as Chancellor and, like von Papen, found his position impossible. After eight weeks he resigned, and President von Hindenburg, with the greatest reluctance, invited Hitler to assume the office of Chancellor, which he did.

Von Papen, who had an idea that he could 'manage' Hitler, became Vice-Chancellor. In this government only two leading cabinet posts were given to Nazis. Wilhelm Frick was appointed Minister of the Interior, and Captain Hermann Goering was made Minister without Portfolio and Minister of the Interior for Prussia. All the other posts went to men chosen by von Hindenburg and von Papen.

It should be understood that Hitler first came into power with perfect legality, as head of a minority party. What put him into office was the hopeless disunity among his opponents, who refused to combine against him. When Hitler took office, the power of the Nazis seemed to be declining; they had lost votes and seats in the November elections.

Hitler decided that he was going to alter all that. What he sought was complete power. He persuaded von Hindenburg to announce the dissolution of the Reichstag and new elections for March 5th.

The time for preparation was short—less than two months. But in this election Hitler had forces at his disposal which he had lacked before. The position of Chancellor enabled him to exercise control over the Government press, the radio, the police. His henchman, Goering, was Minister of the Interior for Prussia, by far the largest German state. At once a ruthless purge began in Prussia; anti-Nazi civil servants and police officials were removed, and their places taken by Nazis. A huge propaganda campaign was started: press and radio blared out announcements that the German nation was in deadly and immediate peril from a vast Jewish-Communist conspiracy. Organized bands of brown-shirts were drafted into the police. They went about the country beating up Jews and Communists, proclaiming that their actions were inspired by patriotism and in the interests of public safety.

These measures were not sufficient. A real scare was needed—some concrete evidence that a conspiracy really existed. What could be more appropriate than the dramatic destruction of an institution which the Nazis intended to destroy anyway?

On the night of February 27th, only six days before the elections, the Reichstag, the great German Parliament building, went up in flames.

The Reichstag was a large, rectangular building, with four towers, and a great central dome beneath which was the parliament chamber, in which the elected members sat. The fire broke out at nine o'clock in the evening, when the streets of Berlin were crowded with people. Before any alarm was given the parliament chamber was a mass of flames, and the glass-domed roof, glowing redly, was a landmark which could be seen for miles.

The circumstances were peculiar. The Germans are an efficient nation: perhaps they are the most efficient nation. Their public services are run with discipline. Is it possible that there were no watchman, guards, or other officials inside the Reichstag at nine in the evening in a time of emergency? Were there no sprinklers, automatic fire alarms, or other fire-prevention devices inside the building? Apparently there were not.

Once the alarm had been given a crowd quickly collected, and fire engines came rushing from all directions. The first member of the government to arrive was Captain Hermann Goering, whose official residence was close to the Reichstag and connected with it by an underground passage. Goering at once gave orders that no newspapermen should be allowed near the building, and that the streets in the neighborhood should be cleared.

During the next twenty minutes hundreds of police,

arriving in trucks or on horseback, cleared the streets, while fifty fire engines assembled to fight the fire. The main blaze was in the wood-panelled parliament chamber, which was almost gutted. But at ten-twenty, when Chancellor Hitler and Vice-Chancellor von Papen came to join Goering, the fire was under control.

Police statements were issued while the Reichstag was still smoking. One story given out was that about twenty different centers of fire had been discovered, consisting of oily rags and wood shavings. The fire, the police said, had undoubtedly been due to incendiarism. At the time of the outbreak a policeman had seen, behind a window, a figure moving about with a torch. He had fired at this figure without hitting him. But a man had been arrested, a young Dutch Communist who had been caught 'setting fire to the Reichstag with his shirt.'

Reporters who pressed for further details were told to wait. The matter was still being investigated. A statement would be issued.

The investigations did not take long. On the 28th, a few hours after the fire, Captain Goering issued his own findings. In a written report he stated:

This act of incendiarism is the most outrageous act yet committed by the Bolsheviks in Germany. The police in their search have uncovered details of plans for a terrorist outbreak on Bolshevik lines. Government buildings, palaces, museums and essential public undertakings were to be set on fire. The burning of the Reichstag was to have been the signal for a bloody uprising and a civil war.

It is established that today acts of terrorism were to have begun all over Germany, directed against individuals, against private property, and against the lives of peaceful citizens.

This explanation roused a lot of skepticism, even in Germany. 'How was it,' asked *Vorwaerts,* the Social Democratic newspaper, 'that this young Dutchman had been able to make all his preparations for setting fire to the Reichstag without attracting any attention?' A story began to circulate that the Nazis themselves had fired the Reichstag.

The answer to this was a series of decrees suspending all articles of the constitution relating to the liberty of the citizen, freedom of the press, and the right of public assembly. The police were empowered to censor private letters, and to enter private houses without search warrants. Justifying these measures Captain Goering told reporters that Adolf Hitler was doing the world a great service with his fight against Communism. The Government, he said, intended to stay in power for a long time, and it was their duty to see that Communism should not be allowed to raise its head again.

The Reichstag Fire, with its accompanying story of a widespread Communist plot, had been Hitler's excuse for seizing power. Some skepticism had been expressed in other countries about the reality of such a plot. A 'Brown Book' had been printed in Belgium in which details of the Reichstag fire conspiracy had been given, but in this version the conspirators had been the Nazis themselves. Some of them, including Goering and Goebbels, had been mentioned by name. The Brown Book, though banned in Germany, had had a wide circulation in other countries. To justify their seizure of power in the eyes of the outside world, the Nazis decided to bring the alleged 'fire conspirators' to trial.

There was a precedent for this decision. During April 1933, the Russians had staged a great public trial of six engineers employed in Russia by the Metropolitan-Vickers Company, and accused of espionage and sabotage. The Russian public prosecutor, a certain Mr. Vishinsky, had been particularly vitriolic in denunciations of the accused. Protesting that the only fair justice in the world was Soviet justice, he had told one of them: 'The only thing you are good for now is to fertilize our Soviet fields.' All the men except one were found guilty and received varying sentences.

In September 1933, when the 'fire conspirators' were brought to trial, it seemed that the Nazi Government was determined to show that anything in the way of public trials which the Russians could do the Nazis could do better. There were five accused. They were:

Marinus van der Lubbe, the young 'Dutch Communist' who had been caught, half-naked, at the scene of the fire.

Ernest Torgler, formerly Chairman of the German Parliamentary Communist Party.

Georgi Dimitroff, a Bulgarian journalist.

Balgoi Popoff, a Bulgarian Communist student.

Wassil Taneff, a Communist shoemaker.

The trial began in Leipzig on September 21st, 1933, and was later transferred to Berlin. It was elaborately staged, with a red-robed judge, hundreds of police and brown-shirts milling about, and a great blare of radio and press publicity. Many celebrated performers took part, including Goebbels and General Goering (who had recently received considerable promotion). Despite unfavorable press notices, it ran for three months, providing entertainment, of a sort, for the whole world.

Van der Lubbe pleaded guilty. He had made a written confession of his guilt. During the greater part of the trial he sat silent, looking half-doped, and, for the most part, refusing to answer questions. His confession was read out to him.

'I laid a fire-lighter under a table covered with cloth and set it on fire. I then lit a curtain separating the restaurant from the west-wing corridor. The floor and doorway began to burn.

'I then took off my coat, waistcoat and shirt, setting fire to my shirt to make a torch, and ran half-naked to the main hall, setting fire to curtains and canopies with the flaming shirt clasped in my hand.

'I ran to the kitchen scullery and set fire to a quantity of linen. I rushed into a lavatory and set fire to twenty-seven face-towels.'

Breaking his sullen silence, van der Lubbe admitted all this, including rushing into the lavatory and setting fire to *twenty-seven* face-towels. But no amount of questioning could make him admit that he had had any accomplices. When questioned he usually remained silent; occasionally he laughed. Asked what he was laughing at, he replied briefly: 'At this trial.'

Torgler and Dimitroff did not remain silent. Nothing could keep them quiet. Their interruptions and satirical observations caused constant scenes of uproar which turned the trial into something resembling one of the wilder efforts of the Marx brothers. The Nazis themselves helped to turn the trial into an utter farce by producing incredible witnesses for the prosecution.

One of them, a convict named Lehman, serving a sentence for theft, had a good story to tell. He claimed that he had belonged to a secret anarchist organization whose members knew each other only by sight, and who were forbidden to greet each other in the street. In 1932, he said, he had gone to Torgler asking for employment, and Torgler had answered: 'I want you for a big job.' This job was to set fire to the Reichstag in such circumstances that the Nazis would appear to have done it. He had virtuously refused this commission because he thought that it would be playing a 'dirty trick' on the Nazis. To this Torgler replied coldly that it was incredible to him that such a man with such a character should be allowed to tell so many lies in the highest German court.

Another witness, a journalist named Zimmern, recalled that a few days before the fire Torgler had told him: 'When the beacon blazes these gentlemen [the Nazis] will creep into their holes.' Asked why he had not reported this conversation on February 27th, but had waited till November 26th to report it, he answered that he had only just realized the importance of it. To this

Torgler retorted: 'Only a little Scherl reporter could state such utter nonsense.' (The publishing house of Scherl was controlled by a prominent Nazi.) After another criminal, convicted of sexual offenses and theft, had given evidence for the prosecution, Dimitroff remarked loudly: 'The chain of evidence for the prosecution, which began with Nazi Deputies and Nazi journalists, is now completed by this thief.'

The trial dragged on and on, one discreditable witness after another giving his evidence. A high-light came on the day on which General (formerly Captain) Goering himself went into the witness box.

His entrance was as carefully produced as that of an opera singer. Cheering crowds lined the streets as he drove to the Court in his huge Mercedes, heavily escorted by armed storm-troopers.

At ten o'clock on the morning of November 4th, General Goering, Premier of Prussia, Reich Air Minister, Speaker of the Reichstag, and General of Reichswehr and Police, entered the court with a large following of uniformed aides and police.

His evidence was simple. He told the court that when, on arrival at the fire, he heard the word arson, 'it was as if a veil had lifted before my eyes. In a moment I knew that the Communists had fired the Reichstag.' He repeated this, saying that he knew 'as if by clairvoyance' that there had been a number of incendiarists, and he warned the court that, whatever verdict they might arrive at, *he* would punish the culprits. To this he added that Hitler had told him that the fire was 'a sign from heaven to show what we should come to if these people ever had power.'

Questioned by Dimitroff, who tried to pin him down to a few facts, he shouted: 'You are a scoundrel who should have been on the gallows long ago.'

As the trial dragged on day after day, and no real evidence was produced against any of the defendants except van der Lubbe, Hitler must have realized that any monstrously unfair verdict would place German justice in the same category as Russian injustice. Whether he took any steps to instruct the court what its verdict should be, is not known. What is known is that he gave strict orders that, whatever the verdict of the court might be, it should be honored.

The court found van der Lubbe guilty, and sentenced him to death. The other four defendants were acquitted.

So ended the Reichstag fire trial. The question is still unanswered: Who fired the Reichstag?

THE GREAT FIRE OF LONDON

1666

THE London of the mid-seventeenth century (population about six hundred thousand) was a busy, crowded and filthy city of low timber-framed houses, churches, and warehouses, clustering about the river Thames. The huge Cathedral of St. Paul's, later rebuilt, set on the height of Ludgate Hill, towered in splendor over the city. First begun in 1087 and not finally completed till 1315, it was 596 feet long by 104 feet wide: the spire rose to a height of nearly five hundred feet.

The city, squatting in the shadow of the great cathedral, was noisy, and it stank. Carts clattered over the narrow, cobbled streets, hawkers shouted from their stalls, and most of the thoroughfares had open, evil-smelling drains. The restoration of the monarchy in 1660 had brought a large influx of population to the city, and in the meaner districts, in the small wooden houses, huddled back to back, families were sleeping six or seven in a room. Beyond the city proper lay the Parliament at Westminster, and the King's Palace at Whitehall, and still farther out were the pretty, rural villages of Knightsbridge and Chelsea.

In 1665 London was ravaged by plague: at one time men and women were dying at the rate of a thousand a week. Many of the richer people left the city. In the autumn of that year the plague died down a little, but in the spring and summer of 1666 it revived, and many more died.

One person who did not leave the city was a rising young civil servant, age 33, named Samuel Pepys. He seems to have been an amiable character and a hard worker, with a passion for music and a strong partiality for women. His job was that of treasurer to the Navy, and he had plenty to keep him busy. During those long, close days of the plague, Mr. Pepys worked hard, enjoyed, whenever possible, the pleasures of music and the table, and went regularly (and sometimes irregularly) to bed. On September 2nd, 1666, he recorded in his diary:

Some of our mayds sitting up late last night to get things ready against our feast to-day. Jane called us up about three in the morning to tell us of a great fire they saw in the city. So I rose and slipped on my night-gowne and went to her and thought it to be on the backside of Marke-Lane: but being unused to such fire as followed I thought it far enough off: and so went to bed and again to sleep.

The fire started very early on a Sunday morning in a tumbledown alley known as Pudding Lane, which ran down to the River Thames near the Tower of London. It was caused by a spark flying from a fire and igniting a pile of brushwood beside the oven in a bakery: the baker's name was Farynor. When flames invaded the upper floor of the house, this man and his wife escaped by climbing out through a window, but a maid, who also lived on the premises, was burned.

For a time the fire attracted little attention. A few neighbors came out of their houses: some half-hearted attempts were made to put the fire out, though nobody seems to have thought of trying to rescue the servant girl. Fires were frequent in that slum area, and people were expected to look after themselves. If they couldn't, nobody else was going to bother about them.

At first the spread of the fire was slow. Then scattered sparks ignited an inn, where the yard and outbuildings were stored with dry hay. The flames seized eagerly on this highly combustible material, and in a few minutes the fire was flaring up tenfold, spreading rapidly along the whole length of the street.

From Pudding Lane the fire spread to Thames Street, near London Bridge, where there were warehouses full of oil, tallow, spirits, and other highly combustible materials brought in by ships unloading at the Port of London. By eight in the morning more than three hundred houses were blazing, and London Bridge was burning down.

The flames, encouraged by a strong north-east wind, roared their way irresistibly along street after street of wooden houses. Little was done to resist their onslaught. Pepys wrote:

. . . and there I did see an infinite great fire on this and the other side of the bridge.

Having staid, and in an hour's time seen the fire rage every way, and nobody, to my sight, endeavouring to quench it, but to remove their goods and leave all to the fire; and having seen it get as far as the Steele-Yard, and the wind mighty high and driving it into the city. . . . I to White Hall and there up to the King's closett in the Chappell, where people did come about me, and I did give them an account which dismayed them all, and word was carried to the King.

The King dispatched troops into the city, and sent a message to the Mayor, by Pepys, instructing him 'to spare no houses but to pull them down before the fire every way.' Still nothing was done, the Lord Mayor arguing that he could not touch houses without the owners' consent. Later houses were pulled down, but too close to the fire, which swept down swiftly on the workmen, driving them away.

That Sunday in September 1666, rumors were spreading across London even more quickly than the fire. It was said that a Dutch force had invaded the city, that the fire was part of a 'Papist Plot,' that paid incendiaries were flinging fireballs into houses, that a great uprising was planned against the peace of the kingdom. Foreigners were manhandled and beaten up in the streets. And still the fire went on spreading. That night Pepys wrote:

We to a little ale house on the Bankside, over against the Three Cranes, and there staid till it was dark almost, and saw the fire grow: and, as it grew darker, appeared more and more, and in corners and upon steeples, and between churches and houses as far as we could see up the hill of the City, in a most horrid, malicious, bloody flame, not like the fine flame of an ordinary fire. We staid till, it being darkish, we saw the fire as only one entire arch of fire from this side to the other side the bridge, and in a bow up the hill for an arch of above a mile long: it made me weep to see it. The churches, houses and all on fire and flaming at once: and a horrid noise the flames made, and the cracking of houses at their ruine.

But worse was to come. The next morning, Monday, September 3rd, was warm and sunny, but with a strong wind still blowing. In the morning the fire, which already covered a wide area along the banks of the river, began to spread quickly to the north, menacing the business heart of the city. Something had to be done, and King Charles abandoning for the time being his menagerie of dogs, came out of his palace at Whitehall and took charge himself, appointing his brother, the Duke of York, his Chief Lieutenant. Whatever defects of character they may have had, neither the King nor his brother lacked courage in an emergency. More militia were called in from the surrounding countryside, fire posts were established, buildings were razed to arrest the progress of the fire, bucket gangs were organized, the King himself leading one of

159

them for a while. But things had been left too long. Whole streets of houses were bursting into flame. John Evelyn, the diarist, wrote in his diary:

Oh the miserable and calamitous spectacle such as haply the world had not seen the like since the foundation of it, nor to be outdone till the universal conflagration. All the sky was of a fiery aspect like the top of a burning oven, the light seene above forty miles round for many nights. God grant my eyes may never behold the like, now seeing above ten thousand houses all in one flame: the fall of houses, towers and churches was like an hideous storme, and the fire all about so hot and inflamed that at last one was not able to approach it, so that they were forced to stand still and let the flames burn on, which they did for neere two miles in length and one in breadth.

Blackfriars, Holborn, Fleet Street—the fire kept on burning. But still St. Paul's Cathedral, towering high over the city in its open churchyard, stood untouched though surrounded by a sea of flames. To many it seemed that a divine hand was protecting it. But there was no protection, even for St. Paul's. With dramatic suddenness flames roared up from the Cathedral roof.

In the space of a few minutes the whole huge building became wrapped in a gigantic cascade of flame. Great stones split apart with the force of explosions: flames spouted from the shattered stained glass windows. From the roof a great river of molten lead gushed downwards,

running along the cobblestones: the great bells fell clanging, and were melted by the intense heat.

Close by, in the vault of St. Faith's, the London book-
sellers had stored their books for safety. Burning timbers
from the great Cathedral ignited this neighboring church,
and books to the value of £150,000, together with all the
valuable books in the library of St. Paul's school, were
destroyed.

For five days the fire burned, destroying fifteen thousand houses, eighty-four churches, and threatening the
Palace of Whitehall itself. Then, on the night of the 5th,
the wind dropped suddenly to a dead calm, and the
wearied soldiers and citizens were able to stop the further
spread of the blaze. But it was a month before the last
small fire, burning in the middle of the ruins, was put out.

Two-thirds of the city was a mass of rubble. Surpris-
ingly, the casualties in human life were very small: the
official figure gives the number as six people killed. But
thousands were homeless. Quoting Evelyn again:

*I then went towards Islington and Highgate, where one
might have seene two hundred thousand people of ranks
and degrees dispersed and lying along by their heapes of
what they could save from the fire, deploring their losse,
and though ready to perish from hunger and destitution,
yet not asking one penny of relief, which to me appeared
a stranger sight than I had yet beheld.*

The King issued a proclamation that food and other
supplies should be given to all the destitute: wagons and

carts began to pour into London from the countryside. A new and statelier London was planned to rise from the ruins. Sir Christopher Wren was asked to produce plans for it.

These plans were rejected, and London began to rise again at the whim of individual builders. Sir Christopher Wren shook his head sadly.

'The citizens of London have proved themselves unworthy of so great a fire,' he said.

THE CHICAGO FIRE

1871

IN 1830 Chicago was a small fort and trading station, situated on the shores of Lake Michigan at a point where the Chicago River ran into the lake. The population was 170. In 1832 the first Sunday School was opened: thirteen children attended.

In 1840 the population was 4,800: the town was going ahead. With the coming of railways the rate of expansion increased vastly. By 1860 Chicago had become the focal point of a vast railway system: the population was then 110,000.

Civil war came, and Chicago contributed large contingents to the victorious Northern armies. And it went on expanding. Some idea of its fantastic rate of expansion can be gained from building figures.

In 1865, seven thousand new buildings were erected, including nine churches, eight schools and colleges, and six public buildings. The cost was 6,950,000 dollars. An enumeration made in 1866 showed that Chicago contained

39,366 buildings, of which 36,654 were of wooden construction, and 3,712 of stone or brick.

Between 1866 and 1871 a total of twenty-three million dollars was spent on construction programs, bringing the total number of buildings up to sixty thousand. During this time the population of the city had risen to 334,000.

Many of the new buildings were on a palatial scale. The new court house was magnificent: the huge office blocks, department stores, opera houses, theaters and hotels could match anything that New York or London had to offer. The elegant homes of Chicago millionaires were full of art treasures. The city had 156 churches: in 1871 the Rev. J. J. Goodspeed, D.D., was able to write: 'Religion, morality, knowledge, culture, and social enjoyments have their seats and temples, paraphernalia and apparatus in as advanced a state of perfection as in any community under the sun.'

The new buildings which were the city's pride were mostly of brick or stone; but the old wooden buildings remained. Even the sidewalks (561 miles of them) were mostly constructed of pine planking. Fires were frequent. After 1870, when Chicago had the record number of seven hundred fires during the year, Lloyd's of London warned their underwriters that fire risks in Chicago should no longer be accepted.

But who cared? If Lloyd's wanted to turn away business, there were plenty of other companies only too ready to do business with a city which had property worth 620 million dollars to insure.

That summer of 1871 had been unusually hot: for fourteen weeks almost no rain had fallen. Fires were burning in the thickly wooded lumber regions of Michigan and Wisconsin. In Chicago the wooden houses were dry and brittle.

On Saturday night, October 7th, a huge fire broke out in Chicago, sweeping across twenty acres of ground and destroying property to the value of seven hundred thousand dollars. The whole of the fire-fighting force of Chicago turned out for this fire, and worked all night and most of the following Sunday subduing the fiercest blaze the city had ever known. By the time this fire was out some thirty firemen, of a total force of 185, had been injured: the remainder were very tired. Some of them, so reports say, were very drunk.

That was the first fire.

The second started on Sunday night October 8th, while the embers of the first were still smoking. It broke out in a tumbledown barn at the back of a building in De Koven Street, and was caused, according to many reports, by an old woman named Mrs. O'Leary, who went into the barn to attend to a sick cow by the light of a kerosene lamp. The cow kicked the lamp over, setting fire to the barn. In a few moments the whole building was ablaze. Before the tired firemen could reach the scene, some thirty buildings were involved.

A violent south-west wind was blowing, carrying burning sparks and embers for long distances and distributing them among bone-dry houses. One of these embers set light to the steeple of St. Paul's Roman Catholic Church, a building a hundred feet long by forty wide. Within a few minutes the whole church collapsed, and sparks and embers rose from it as if from a volcano.

Next door to the church a large furnishing plant flashed into flame with the force of an explosion. There was another great flare-up as a 240-foot-long shingle mill went up with a great roar. Firemen, helpless against the swift onrush of the flames, had to abandon their equipment to save their lives.

Eye-witnesses have given graphic accounts of the early and rapid spread of the fire. One wrote:

The people of the quarter through which the fire first passed were of a class the most likely to be careless in the extreme. In that quarter were the low brothels of Griswold, Jackson and Wells Streets, as well as the more showy haunts of vice on more respectable streets, and the rooms of kept mistresses in upper stories of business blocks. Awakened from their slumbers or aroused from the orgies by the near approach of the flames which travelled like lightning from house to house, the denizens of that inflammable quarter, half-clad for the most part, had barely time to escape and rush pell-mell into the street.

The people were mad. They stumbled over broken furniture and fell and were trampled underfoot. Seized with wild and causeless panics they surged together backwards and forwards in the narrow streets, cursing, threatening, imploring to get free. Villainous, haggard with debauch . . . they smashed windows and with bloody fingers rifled impartially till, shelf, and cellar, fighting viciously for the spoils of their forays. Liquor flowed like water, for the saloons were broken open and despoiled and men on all sides could be seen frenzied with drink.

On Adams Street, not far from the church, a big gas-works was threatened. The night engineer at his post in the control room, fearing an explosion, went around opening valves which controlled the flow of gas to the various pipelines, letting the gas escape into the sewers. This gas, coming up through manholes, started more fires.

Soon after midnight the flames crossed the river, advancing towards the business district. To use the words of an eye-witness:

So the fearful pyrotechnic wall, seething with the power of an inborn indescribable calidity [heat] *and towering upwards more than a hundred feet, came rumbling down to the banks of the river near Twelfth Street, and at a single bound crossed over the river to destroy the heart of Chicago's business life.*

People were now driven from elegant residences, from the upper floors of business houses, from hotels, from lofts. . . . Still the colossal besom of that holocaust swept down towards them with terrific speed, presenting the appearance of a great wall of towering brass and increasing its altitude as it devoured block after block of towering edifices. Many a man and woman sank to the earth in sore affright, many from utter exhaustion, and some from hopelessness of their ability to escape the impending catastrophe. The streets were constantly filled by reinforcements to this mad chase and frequently so tightly wedged by the great mass of humanity that the weak were trampled, bruised, and some killed outright. Persons conveying valuables were ruthlessly despoiled of them: even women and children were robbed of shawls, cloaks and trinkets and outrageously abused by the mob of thieves and roughs that now came like so many vultures to their prey.

Another eye-witness described the fire as seen from the residential part of the town. He wrote:

Called from their beds to witness the fire upon the south side of the river, the people of the quiet and elegant residence-quarter east of Clark and south of Superior Streets, were gazing at the magnificent spectacle and uttering their exclamations of pity for the unfortunate inhabitants across the river, when they found, to their horror, that the flames had already been communicated to their own quarter and that the water-works and other buildings to the rear of them were ablaze.

A terrible panic ensued. There was a sudden screaming and dashing about of half-clad women gathering up such valuables as could be suddenly snatched. Then there was a rush through the streets, some of the wild faces pushing eagerly in this direction and others quite as eagerly in the opposite; and children screaming; and brands falling in showers; and truckmen running each other down; and half-drunken wholly desperate ruffians seizing valuables and insulting women; and oaths from lips unused to them as hot as the flames which leaped and crackled nearby.

The destruction of the waterworks is described in these words:

The flying brands and sparks set fire to the roof immediately above the engine-room, the farthest point from the sweeping ocean of flame that had already travelled three miles in six hours. This was instantly extinguished, but soon after the great breweries nearby burst into roaring flames and tongues of fire were darting over the turreted roof of the waterworks building. Within, the atmosphere became heated to a degree that made it impossible for the workmen and engineers to perform their duty. Then the immense roof crumbled in upon the three mammoth engines.

And the Court House:

Far north of Van Buren Street the fire licked up gigantic squares of marble palaces and approached the Court House. This splendid building occupied the center of a square, and owing to its isolated situation and its being surrounded by fireproof buildings was considered free from danger. But even before the sea of flames surrounded it, the ruthless wind hurled flaming brands and sparks upon the great dome, and the edifice was soon a mass of flames. The watchman started the machinery that tolled the ponderous bell and fled from the building: the bell boomed forth the news of the terrible catastrophe, until the vast dome tottered, reeled, and fell crashing into the interior with all its weight of several million pounds.

169

The prisoners in the jail were released, and at once celebrated their freedom by looting a nearby jewelry store.

Thousands of people took refuge on the sandy beach of the lake, or in a park north of the city, where twenty-four hours of exposure awaited them. Without food or drink, and with the pitiless cinders continually raining down, their plight was miserable.

The fire went on. In the words of an eye-witness:

The task of following its course or describing its ravages in detail became an utter impossibility. Everybody was mad, and everything was hell. The earth and sky were fire and flames: the atmosphere was smoke. A perfect hurricane was blowing, and drew the fiery billows with a screech through roads and alleys, between the tall buildings, as if it were sucking them through a tube: great sheets of flames flapped in the air. The sidewalks were all ablaze and the fire ran along them as fast as a man could walk. Roofing became detached in great sheets and drove down the sky like huge blazing arrows. There was fire everywhere, underfoot, overhead, around. It ran along tindery roofs, it sent out curling wisps of blue smoke from under eaves, it smashed glass with an angry crackle and gushed out in a torrent of red and black: it climbed in delicate tracery up the fronts of buildings, licking up with a serpent tongue little bits of woodwork: it broke through roofs with a rattling rush and hung out blood-red signals of victory. The flames were of all colors, pale pink, golden, scarlet, crimson, blood-hued amber. The flames advanced like a great army.

The first really determined attempt to fight the fire was made by another army. United States troops, under the command of General Sheridan, began to blow up whole streets of houses to stop the spread of the fire. In this their efforts were partially successful. They succeeded in stopping the spread of the flames towards the south. Help was also coming in from other cities: engines and fire-fighting equipment were being brought by rail and water from Milwaukee, Cincinnati, Dayton. Later in the afternoon the wind velocity slackened, and a slight rain fell. The spread of the fire was checked. Among the ruins small fires would go on smouldering for days, but the worst was over.

In twenty-four hours of fire, 250 people had been killed, and seventeen thousand buildings burned. Most of the business section of Chicago had been entirely wiped out: damage to the value of 168 million dollars had been done. Rich men had become paupers in a night and a day. Ninety thousand people of all classes were homeless, crowded in hastily improvised refugee camps, or in the open, owning only what they had on, waiting for somebody to feed them. 'The vilest crusts,' a reporter wrote, 'have now become sweet morsels to the pampered children of luxury. The fashionable belle forgets the length of her train and the style of her chignon in the merciless gnawing of hunger, and joins the eleemosynary throng without a care for the opinion of society, anxious to satisfy the demands of nature at any sacrifice of pride.'

Help was quick in arriving. Trainloads of food and clothing were at once rushed towards Chicago, and huge subscriptions for relief of the sufferers were raised in many American cities. Within a few days more than two million dollars had been collected, and more was to come in. Large subscriptions were also raised in Europe. A Mansion House fund in London exceeded two hundred thousand dollars, and such cities as Birmingham, Liverpool, Manchester and Sheffield also sent large donations to Chicago.

A few days after the fire sixty American insurance companies went into bankruptcy: these included fourteen in the State of Illinois and twenty in New York. They simply hadn't anything like the money needed to meet the claims against them. According to the New York *Spectator*, claims against insurance companies totalled ninety million dollars, of which only about thirty-five million was actually paid. The largest insurance liability to be met promptly and in full was that of three and a half million dollars by the Liverpool, London and Globe Insurance Company of London: the second largest was two million dollars which was paid by the North British and Mercantile Company, also of London.

'The cow that burned a city' featured prominently in the world's newspapers, and street traders did a brisk business in relics: thousands of pieces of skin, tail, bones, and horn were sold, all purported to have come from Mrs. O'Leary's cow. One enterprising gentleman went on a lecture tour, taking with him a cow and a kerosene lamp which, he claimed, had started the fire.

The Rev. Granville Moody, of the Methodist Church of Cincinnati (reported in the *New York Tribune* of

October 20th, 1871) told his congregation that he had no doubt whatever that the calamity which had befallen Chicago could be attributed to the fact that the city had recently given a majority vote against the observation of the Sabbath and the liquor laws, and was also a retributive judgment on a city which had shown such devotion in its worship of the Golden Calf. He warned his congregation that their own city was in considerable danger.

This view was disputed by authors Elias Colbert and Everett Chamberlain. In their book, *Chicago And The Great Conflagration* (F. C. Vent, Cincinnati and New York, 1872) they stated: 'If Chicago had been destroyed by an earthquake or volcano, or any other convulsion of the elements . . . it might have been called a special judgment of Heaven: but coming in a way which made one only wonder why it had not come before, it cannot be construed otherwise than as a timely reminder of God, working through the elements, and as a hint to fear Him, love our fellowmen, subdue our pride, and make our walls of brick, eschewing wooden roofs. A fireproof building is perhaps as proper a monument to the superiority of the Divine power as any we can raise.'

If the fire had been terrible, the behavior of the citizens of Chicago, *after the fire*, was admirable. Before the ashes of the burned-out buildings were cold, they had started rebuilding. Within a month more than 1,400 houses had been put up, and business was being done in temporary wooden structures on the sites of burned-down stores and offices. Within three days of its offices and printing works being gutted, the *Chicago Tribune* was for sale again on the streets of Chicago in a small edition with a banner headline: 'Chicago shall rise.' In England, *Punch*, appealing for subscriptions to the Mansion House fund, warned its readers to send their subscriptions in quickly or the city would be rebuilt before the money reached it.

Summing-up the possibilities of a glowing future for Chicago, the Rev. E. J. Goodspeed wrote: 'The principal temptation of city life should be put away by the absolute prohibition of all sales of intoxicating liquor. Gambling should be made a crime: harlotry should be trampled under foot: the Sabbath should be regarded as a sacred institution. Literature and art should be made to minister, not, as in Paris, to the worse portions of our nature, but to the ennobling, gratification, refinement, and culture of the whole community.

'Immense engines and accessible reservoirs should be provided by which whole blocks could be flooded. . . . The Fire Department should be organized and drilled to an efficiency like that attained among soldiers of the regular army.

'Then . . . our influence would extend wherever it was felt that the tone of public sentiment would be exalted and our example would be such that the Republic, energized and purified, would pulsate with new life and her glorious career would prolong itself to the end of time.'

THE SAN FRANCISCO FIRE

1906

UNLIKE Chicago, San Francisco was not a new city. In 1579 Sir Francis Drake anchored close to the entrance to the Bay, and claimed the surrounding country for Queen Elizabeth, naming it Nova Albion. After he sailed away his visit was forgotten, and San Francisco passed into the possession of Spain, and then of Mexico. Finally, in 1846, after a brief war between the United States and Mexico, the United States took it.

During the next sixty years the population increased from about a thousand to almost half a million people. The San Francisco of 1906 was not only a busy city. It was, from all accounts, a gay and friendly city, loved by writers and artists. Money was made quickly, and spent quickly. San Francisco had everything—a wonderful climate, lovely surroundings, luxurious hotels and impressive business premises, superb art galleries and libraries. Nothing was too good for San Francisco.

At five-fifteen on the morning of April 18th, 1906, the city was sleeping. Lights winked here and there. A few late-night revellers were staggering home: a few early ris-

175

ers were already going to work: but the greater part of the population was asleep.

The peace of the city was abruptly disturbed by a sickening commotion as houses and public buildings swayed violently under a severe earthquake. The ground beneath the city seemed to be undulating in waves. Beds slid across floors, pictures and china fell, walls collapsed, buildings tumbled: from everywhere came a sound of grinding and banging, mingled with shrill, frightened screams and the crash of breaking glass. Watchers, from a distance, saw the lights of the city go out suddenly. The earthquake had severed the gas and electricity mains.

The earthquake was brief, lasting only a minute and a half, but it brought down a number of buildings and opened gaping cracks across many streets. The air was thick with dust from falling masonry.

In a few moments the streets were jammed by a mob of choking and panic-stricken people, many of them half-clad. Roused from sleep by the horrible swaying of the earth, they came pouring out of homes, hotels, wooden shanties, milling about in the darkness in utter bewilderment, unable to understand what was happening. Many thought that the end of the world had come.

Before the terrified crowds had time to gather their wits, the darkness was relieved by the red glare of flames as fires broke out all over the city. Police and firemen turned out, shouting and bawling, trying to force a passage for the fire engines through seething mobs of people. Their efforts were to prove heart-breakingly futile. When the firemen coupled their hoses and opened the valves from the hydrants, no water came through. The shock which had severed the gas mains and electric cables, thus causing the fires, had also severed the water mains.

The firemen did their utmost under the circumstances. Sewage water was used: thousands of gallons of it were pumped onto the flames. But it was not enough. There were too many fires, burning in too many places: there were too few firemen and too little water to deal with an outbreak of fires on such a scale. And in the poorer quarters ('shanty town') there were too many wooden buildings, providing the fuel the fire needed to enable it to sweep with devastating force into the more solidly built streets and thoroughfares.

The story of the Chicago fire of 1871 began to repeat itself on an even bigger scale. The city burned. Fanned by a strong wind, the flames spread rapidly, one fire joining with another to make a conflagration a mile and a half long by half a mile deep. As the fire advanced, men and women fled before it. Wild-eyed people of many nationalities were trying frantically to rescue a few cherished possessions, dragging bales, bundles, suitcases, and even solid pieces of furniture through the streets. Many who had rushed out at the first shock, and then run back into their houses to try to save what they could, were trapped in their homes. People retreating hastily from one fire would turn a corner to find themselves confronted by another.

As had happened in Chicago forty-five years earlier, hordes of looters broke into stores and residential districts, drinking and robbing. Some were shot. Others, obsessed by their greed, were caught in the flames, and died with their pockets stuffed with stolen property. The mayor issued a proclamation authorizing soldiers and police to *kill* any and all persons found looting.

By mid-morning the whole of San Francisco was overhung by a pall of black smoke. Through this smoke flaming brands and large pieces of timber were whirled up into the air, to fall great distances away and start other fires. This is a feature common to huge conflagrations like those of Chicago and San Francisco: it is caused by hot air rising and creating a tremendous updraught.

Soldiers were brought in to use dynamite to make firestops, but their efforts were ineffective. So great was the radiated heat that the fire jumped gaps made by dynamited buildings and burned on unchecked.

One by one the great office buildings and hotels crumbled before the fire. Parks and beaches were crowded with thousands of refugees, clutching their few possessions. At night the glow from the burning city could be seen fifty miles away.

Two days passed before the fire finally burned itself out. In that time it had devastated four square miles of the city, burned twenty-eight thousand buildings, and killed 452 people. The damage was estimated at one billion dollars—five times the damage caused by the Chicago fire.

Relief trains poured into the stricken city, and with them came hundreds of tramps and criminals, eager for whatever valuables might be lying about among the ruins. Strong measures had to be taken: a curfew was imposed, and at night the streets were patrolled by armed police and soldiers.

And then, as had happened in Chicago, the citizens set to work to rebuild their city. Within a week business was being done among the ruins: within a year an extensive building program was in full swing. Within four years a new San Francisco had risen, statelier, more beautiful, and far more fireproof than the old one.

THE KANTO EARTHQUAKE AND FIRE
(TOKYO AND YOKOHAMA)

1923

FOR sheer violence and destructive power the Kanto earthquake and fire in Japan in 1923 is probably the worst single disaster ever recorded in history. The San Francisco earthquake in 1906 lasted for one and a half minutes. In the Kanto earthquake 1,700 shocks followed one another with diminishing ferocity over a period of days. An area of forty-five thousand square miles was ploughed up as if a giant tractor had run over it. Hills disappeared: valleys were filled with debris and shattered buildings: the countryside was littered with wreckage. Among the cities laid in ruins were Tokyo and Yokohama.

The first shocks began in Tokyo at about noon on Saturday, September 1st, 1923. They were extremely violent. As the ground swirled and heaved, there was a hideous grinding and crashing as thousands of houses collapsed, the walls falling outwards and the roofs inwards, burying great numbers of people in their ruins. With the shocks continuing, a vast dust-cloud arose, wrapping the city in a gritty twilight. Almost immediately fires began burning all over Tokyo.

Out of the jumbled confusion of overturned cars and carts, and the splintered ruins of houses, men and women crawled, with the earth still swaying beneath them. Streets and thoroughfares had almost ceased to exist. Flames, sweeping through the dry, piled-up wreckage of the flimsy houses, were mounting higher and higher, with nothing to check them.

There was little panic. One feature which struck every foreign observer of this catastrophe was the extraordinary courage displayed by men and women alike. With flames hemming them in, and buildings still falling, men and women worked doggedly in the wreckage, trying to extricate friends and relatives. Many perished while trying to save others.

As the flames swallowed entire districts of the city, refugees began to stream away to open spaces. A crowd estimated to number between thirty and forty thousand people took refuge in the grounds formerly occupied by an army clothing depot on the eastern bank of the river Sumida. This area became the center of a roaring inferno of flames, from which there was no escape, and these people were killed.

The flames slowly died down, but the thick cloud of dust seemed to form a permanent twilight in the stricken city. A correspondent wrote: 'The ruins of the city are a waste of hot tiles and masonry, giving off clouds of gritty dust and the stench of burned bodies. In the busi-

181

iness quarter I was able to recognize business offices simply by the rows of iron safes standing in the ashes.'

Many Europeans were staying in the Imperial Hotel in Tokyo at that time. This hotel, designed to be earthquake-proof, had opened only a few days before the earthquake. The designer was the American architect, Frank Lloyd Wright.

The hotel was built in the form of a letter H, and founded on huge concrete pontoons, which could move with the movement of the earth. When the earthquake struck Tokyo, the hotel rolled like a ship. But it stood, and continued to give service and meals during the entire emergency.

A friend of mine was staying at the Imperial. He has described to me how the Japanese, while the city was still smoking, were already clearing things up. Many of them were injured. There was no food, and very little water. And there were no complaints. When a new earthquake shock came they simply stopped what they were doing. When it had passed they went on working.

Tokyo was only one incident in this disaster. In Yokohama, with the first quake, most of the houses collapsed. As in Tokyo, fire at once swept through the town. With the continuing shocks, vast chasms were opened in the ground, in which many perished. Others were blinded by smoke and dust, and went about aimlessly, not knowing where they were going.

The dead were heaped in the streets, and in the canal and harbor hundreds of bodies were floating on the surface of the water. Between Tokyo and Yokohama a trail of wreckage and desolation extended over the whole countryside. Dazed survivors, moving mutely about an unrecognizable landscape, searched for relatives. In one place, a railway train, thrown bodily from the line by the first shock, lay in a tangled pile of wreckage and corpses by the side of the track.

Epidemics of typhus and dysentery broke out, caused by contaminated water supplies. Government forces moved in and took over the direction of affairs: martial law was proclaimed. Thousands of bodies were dragged out of the ruins and burned in enormous crematoria.

In Tokyo (population 2,031,300) more than three hundred thousand houses had been destroyed. In Yokohama seventy thousand buildings had gone. The casualties over the whole earthquake and fire area reached the colossal total of a million and a half people, of whom two hundred thousand were dead.

You have been reading a book about notable fires. Certain friends to whom I showed the manuscript of this book told me that, since reading it, whenever they go into a restaurant or theater, the first thing they do is to look around nervously to see if there is any quick way of getting out. That is certainly an exaggeration. The only people likely to suffer from a nervous dread of fire as the result of reading a book are those people who are subject to nervous dreads anyway.

Without being morbid about sickness, most sensible people take certain precautions against it. At least they insist on their children being warmly clad in cold weather, and make them change their clothes when they get wet. The same people very often use unguarded fires, or overload their electric circuits, thus running the risk of burning their families to death. It seems a little crazy.

Fires are with us all the time, and every year the figures of casualties and damage seem to grow larger. In the United States fire damage in 1957 cost the country almost a billion dollars. Most of the fires which caused this damage were preventable. They need not have happened.

There have been other large fires while I was writing

185

this book. In December 1956, while I was writing about explosions, there was a large explosion at the Luckenbach pier, in Brooklyn: several people were killed. In January, 1957, while I was writing about bush fires, there were great fires burning in California and Australia. There has been a fire in the Jaguar Motor Company's plant in Coventry, England. Damage is estimated at three and a half million pounds. Production (at the time of writing) was held up, and four thousand men were idle for days.

There have been similar fires.

On August 12th, 1953, in the biggest industrial fire loss ever recorded, a plant covering thirty-five acres and belonging to the General Motors Corporation, at Livonia, Michigan, was destroyed by fire. The flat roof, covering an area of about one and a half million square feet, was covered with a 'bituminous' material. This roof melted, and the fire spread over the whole plant. Three men were killed.

So it goes on, but this book has to come to an end.

Some of the personal opinions which I have expressed in this book may be regarded as debatable, but all personal opinions are debatable. The facts I have set down are as accurate as I have been able to make them. It is seldom that several reports of any occurrence correspond exactly in detail, and I have read through numerous reports of all the fires which I have described. I hope that a considerable experience of sifting intelligence reports and preparing appreciations of military situations during the war has enabled me to attain a fairly high degree of accuracy.